FOR THE BEAUTY
OF THE EARTH

FOR THE BEAUTY OF THE EARTH

Women, Sacramentality, and Justice

SUSAN A. ROSS

**2006 Madeleva Lecture
in Spirituality**

PAULIST PRESS
New York/Mahwah, New Jersey

Book and cover design by Lynn Else

Copyright © 2006 by Saint Mary's College, Notre Dame, Indiana

The quotation by Annie Dillard is from her book *For the Time Being* (New York: Vintage Books, 1999), 65–66.

The quotation by Ann Patchett is from her book *Truth and Beauty: A Friendship* (New York: HarperCollins, 2004), 11–12. Used with permission.

Library of Congress Cataloging-in-Publication Data

Ross, Susan A.
    For the beauty of the earth : women, sacramentality, and Justice / Susan A. Ross.
        p. cm.—(Madeleva lecture in spirituality ; 2006)
    Includes bibliographical references.
    ISBN 0-8091-4422-0 (alk. paper).
    1. Aesthetics—Religious aspects—Christianity. 2. Feminist theology. 3. Feminine beauty (Aesthetics) 4. Nature (Aesthetics) 5. Nature—Religious aspects—Christianity. I. Title. II. Series.
    BR115.A8R69 2006
    230.082—dc22
                                                                2006010351

Published by Paulist Press
997 Macarthur Boulevard
Mahwah, New Jersey 07430

www.paulistpress.com

Printed and bound in the United States of America

of the Earth FOR THE BEAUTY OF THE EARTH **FOR THE BEAUTY OF THE EARTH** For the Beauty of the Earth FOR THE BEAUTY OF THE EARTH **FOR THE BEAUTY OF THE EARTH** For the Beauty of the Earth FOR THE BEAUTY OF THE EARTH **FOR THE BEAUTY OF THE EARTH** For the Beauty of the Earth FOR THE BEAUTY OF THE EARTH **FOR THE BEAUTY OF THE EARTH** For the Beauty of the Earth FOR THE BEAUTY OF THE EARTH **FOR THE BEAUTY OF THE EARTH** For the Beauty of the Earth FOR THE BEAUTY OF THE EARTH **FOR THE BEAUTY OF THE EARTH** For the Beauty of the Earth FOR THE BEAUTY OF THE EARTH **FOR THE BEAUTY OF THE EARTH** For the Beauty of the Earth FOR THE BEAUTY OF THE EARTH **FOR THE BEAUTY OF THE EARTH** For the Beauty of the Earth FOR THE BEAUTY OF THE EARTH **FOR THE BEAUTY OF THE EARTH** For the Beauty of the Earth FOR THE BEAUTY OF THE EARTH **FOR THE BEAUTY OF THE EARTH** For the Beauty of the Earth FOR THE BEAUTY OF THE EARTH **FOR THE BEAUTY OF THE EARTH** For the Beauty of the Earth FOR THE BEAUTY OF THE EARTH **FOR THE BEAUTY OF THE EARTH** For the Beauty of the Earth FOR THE BEAUTY OF

Dr. Susan A. Ross is professor of theology and a faculty scholar at Loyola University Chicago. She received her doctorate from the University of Chicago. She is the author of *Extravagant Affections: A Feminist Sacramental Theology* (New York: Continuum, 1998), the coeditor (with Maureen A. Tilley) of *Broken and Whole: Essays on Religion and the Body* (University Press of America, 1995), and the author of numerous journal articles and book chapters on such topics as women and the Eucharist, embodiment, feminist theology, and feminist ethics. She is the recipient of a Louisville Institute Sabbatical Grant, the Book of the Year Award from the College Theology Society in 1999, and the Ann O'Hara Graff Award of the Women's Seminar of The Catholic Theological Society of America.

Dr. Ross wishes to thank Loyola University Chicago for giving her a Reseach Stimulation Award to assist her in finishing this manuscript.

CONTENTS

Preface ix

  I. Beauty and Justice at Home 1

 II. Women, Beauty, and the Church . . 32

III. Women, Beauty, and Justice
in the World 61

Notes 89

In memory of my mother
Mary Flynn Ross Griffin

1923–2000

PREFACE

In the world of academic theology, the last decade has seen a surge of interest in theological aesthetics, as the work of Hans Urs von Balthasar and his disciples has become more widely known, and as other theologians find themselves drawn to ideas of the good, the true, and the beautiful. Catholic and Protestant authors have joined their Orthodox colleagues with a renewed interest in icons. Even scientists describe the cosmos in the language of beauty. Yet, with a very few exceptions, this work takes little notice of women's perspectives on beauty. Even though feminist scholars have contributed to nearly every discipline imaginable, their ways of rethinking scholarly discourse have not had a noticeable effect in the field of theological aesthetics.

It would be easy to dismiss this situation, as theological aesthetics may seem to occupy a highly specialized or arcane niche in the world of theology. Few feminist theologians take on the considerable opus of von Balthasar, and his reputation for conservatism, at least with regard to gender issues, is well deserved.[1] But for feminist theologians to ignore the role of beauty in theology would be a mistake, for at least three reasons. First, feminist theology contains an explicit although undeveloped theological aesthetics, as feminist theologians' scrutiny of the multiplicity of images of God and of humanity is at the same time a focus on the ways in which men and women respond both intellectually and emotionally to the symbols and metaphors of their tradition. Such work inevitably involves the aesthetic. Second, the field of theological aesthetics has tended either to romanticize or, less often, to demonize the feminine as a symbol of heavenly or profane beauty. This use of the feminine needs critical examination and critique, since these conceptions of beauty often have little to do with women's real lives. Third, women's contributions to the beauty of the earth have gone unnoticed and unappreciated, as feminist art historians have noted for some time. Although there have been a few references to women's "crafts"—often not credited as "art"—much more needs to be done to retrieve and restore women's works of art as ways of glorifying God.

These reflections attempt to begin to fill the gap in this literature. It is significant that in recent years attention has shifted away from theological method and the limits of rational explorations of theology to beauty. It is important to (re)value theologically what touches our senses and hearts as well as what challenges our thinking. And it is even more important to engage in this retrieval with attention to the ways in which gender has played a role, both in the present and in the past. For too long God's hidden-yet-revealed presence in the world, which the Christian tradition has named sacramental, has found itself more often in men's ways of seeing and doing than women's. It is both appropriate and just that women's ways of seeing and doing be valued as well.

I begin with women's experiences of beauty with regard to their persons and their homes, in some of the more intimate ways in which issues of beauty arise. It may come as a surprise to some that personal beauty and home design can serve as material for theological reflection. Yet, because women have not had full access to the public and sacred spaces of human life, women have used their creative energies in the places where they can. I next turn to the space of the church and explore the ways in which women's concern for beauty has indeed had an effect on our officially designated sacred spaces, although not in the ways that have been most remembered or documented. Finally, I turn to the wider world and note how women's desire for beauty has found its way into their communities and the natural world.

Throughout these reflections I have drawn on my own experiences and on what I have learned from others, as the previous Madeleva lecturer, Mary Ann Hinsdale, has invited women theologians to do. I have learned a great deal about beauty from women, and particularly from my mother. It is to her memory that this Madeleva lecture is dedicated.

I

BEAUTY AND JUSTICE AT HOME

I first began to think seriously about the connection between beauty and justice during the five years I lived in a condominium on the far north side of Chicago. My neighborhood seemed always to be fighting a losing battle against the forces of ugliness and violence. Our small six-flat condo building was one of the few bright spots on a block that was marginal, at best. One of the owners spent hours landscaping our tiny front yard. He planted flowers around the bases of the two trees, and put in small white picket fences to protect them. But the flowers got trampled, and the fence was torn. Some of the neighbors threw their garbage onto the sidewalk. My car's hood was dented by the young men who used it for a bench. I was repeatedly awakened by foul language coming from the alley next to my windows, and I came to dread warm weather, since the noise and litter seemed to increase with every degree. Late one summer night, I came home alone after a party and was mugged in the vestibule of our building. Four months later

I sold my condo and moved to a much smaller and more expensive rental apartment in a nearby suburb. I felt both guilt and relief after the move: guilt because I felt I had abandoned my solidarity with the poor, and relief because I felt safe. I was now surrounded by beauty: well-maintained homes, carefully tended lawns, trees, flowers, quiet. I felt better able to work, calmer and more optimistic, and better able to tackle the challenges of life. I felt whole. I kept thinking, though, of the people in the neighborhood I had left behind.

Was there a connection between my new feeling of well-being and my surroundings? Of course there was. And was there a connection as well between the ugliness of my old neighborhood and the ugliness of some people's actions? I think there is. It seemed to me then, as it still does, that what it takes to be a good person is not simply "doing the right thing" because it *is* the right thing. Sometimes that is the case, of course. Stories of the courage and selflessness of people in terrible situations of poverty or cruelty tell us that our external conditions do not wholly determine our actions. But often these are the exceptions. So I have been pursuing these questions over the last few years—questions about our desires, feelings, and environments and their relation to our senses of goodness and justice.

I have had a lifelong love for the arts, especially music, and wrote my doctoral dissertation on the relationship between aesthetic and religious understandings of truth. My book on the sacraments explored the ways in which women's actions, while not explicitly or officially sacramental, nevertheless have a powerful sacramental quality that could and should inform our thinking and practice of the sacraments. My questions about beauty and justice connect with my interest in women's lives and concerns, since it is women who are most often identified with beauty, women who are seen to concern themselves—sometimes to an extreme—with beauty, and women who deal with beauty on a very mundane level. Although things have changed somewhat over the last thirty or forty years with the influence of the women's movement, still women have largely not been the ones who have defined beauty or theorized about beauty. Rather, women *are* beauty. It seems that in many accounts of beauty, women just need to be beautiful, for others.

There is, I believe, a connection between beauty and justice. I am not the first, nor will I be the last, to make such a connection. But little has been said about the wisdom and experiences of women over the millennia who have been making themselves, their families, and their homes beautiful; they have something important, I think, to teach us. And while in recent years some theologians have turned to various theologies of beauty, they have done so largely ignoring the contributions of

3

women. Indeed, in these theories, women have been more a symbolic *icon of* beauty than either *perceivers or makers* of beauty, a point I will pursue later.[2] In this work, I will explore the ways in which women's experiences of beauty in themselves, in their homes, in church, and in the wider society tell us some important things about God's sacramental presence in the world. Yet, this presence is not a static one: we are all called to make the world a better place and, yes, a more beautiful place. For beauty and justice are indeed connected. We are drawn to do the good because it is true and beautiful.

In this first part, I will take a close look at how beauty and justice are linked in the private spaces of our lives: in our persons, our homes, and our immediate surroundings. It will surely come as no surprise to anyone that the beauty of one's personal appearance and of one's home have traditionally been the realm of women. While there are now some fashion magazines geared toward men (e.g., *GQ, Maxim*) and while more men are having cosmetic surgery and buying personal-care products than ever before,[3] women are still the vast majority of the purchasers of so-called beauty products. My effort will be to probe a little deeper here—more than skin-deep, so to speak—and consider what women's efforts to be beautiful and to make their homes beautiful can tell us, both positively and negatively.

Five and a half years ago, when my mother died, the pastor of her church preached the homily at her funeral. I can't remember everything he said, but his main point was that when my mother came to church each week, she was always dressed beautifully, as if she were going to a very elegant dinner party—which, in fact, she was, in a manner of speaking. My mother did not own a single pair of jeans. And when my husband and I got married one October, she was aghast at my (I thought clever) idea that we would have miniature pumpkins at our tables with markers for the guests to make bride and groom pumpkins. She ordered beautiful floral centerpieces for us instead. From my mother, I have inherited a love of music and something of an eye for beauty, pumpkins aside! And what I learned from her was that appearances do matter, but not in the way one might think. From my mother, and others along the way, I have learned that beauty is to be shared, that creating beauty is a statement that one cares about others and about one's self—not so much that others will think the wrong thing, but rather that they are worth the time and effort to be cared for, with attention to the details. Ultimately, beauty's power to draw us in and beyond ourselves is a significant element—indeed, a necessary element—in our moral development. And, I would also venture, the beauty of the world gives us a sense of the care

5

with which God holds us, a care that is attuned to our senses and to our, and God's, delight.

As a teenager and into my twenties, I never thought of myself as beautiful. I always thought my three sisters to be far more attractive than I was. But I gradually learned that my own internal image of myself matched what I felt myself to be externally: not beautiful. And as I came to see myself as a good and worthy person, I began to pay more attention to how I presented myself to the world: that I cared about myself, that I had a good appearance. I consider myself fortunate that I never felt that my life or my success depended upon my looks, and I find it truly unfortunate that the ideas of personal beauty that drive our society convey this message all too strongly. But I came to see that while looks were definitely not everything, looking good was not a bad thing. Feminism, contrary to popular perceptions, is not anti-beauty.

Most of us are familiar, I think, with the feminist criticism of fashion-magazine standards of beauty. Yet these criticisms, while important and necessary, may unwittingly overlook the fact that we are embodied creatures and thus we depend on our physicality. In fact, our senses seem to have some kind of innate sense of beauty that we share with other living species: we are drawn to the plumage and song of birds, the softness of animal fur, the aroma of flowers, the tastes of ripe fruit. All of these appeal not only to discriminating humans, but also to very discriminating animals, birds, and even insects. So although there is a very real ambiguity in beauty, in that we may only initially see or experience one of its dimensions, real beauty signifies a depth beyond its appearance.

In this first part, I will develop three ideas related to women, beauty, and justice. The first is that we are in some ways "hard-wired" for beauty and for novelty. Beauty is not an "add-on" to what it means to be a living being; it is, rather, partly constitutive of who we are. Thus we need to ask about its integration into our lives and its role in our moral deliberations and development, particularly for women. Second, we lack helpful models for linking beauty and justice; indeed, we lack models for beauty that are not extreme, on one or the other side of a pendulum. Given this lack of adequate models or examples, it is no surprise that we find it difficult to sort out our thinking and feeling about beauty and justice. So our second task will be to see if there are some helpful base points to construct such an example. Third, I will develop the point that real beauty in relation to the self and the home is connected with generosity and self-love. To the extent that we find it difficult to love ourselves, we find it difficult to see the beauty in ourselves, to share what we have, and to exaggerate the beauty we may perceive in others. Thus we need to develop a model of self-love that incorporates beauty. Such a love will increase our care for and generosity to others as well as ourselves.

The "Naturalness" of Beauty

It is easy to consider the role of beauty in the so-called natural world. Any one of us can think of beautiful scenery, flowers, sunsets, the songs of birds. When I think of spectacular natural beauty, I think of the time a friend and I spent two days hiking in Yosemite, or the time my husband and I drove through the Austrian Alps, or when I spent two weeks in Africa and saw Mount Kilimanjaro rising above the fields in Tanzania. But it is also easy to romanticize this beauty and to see only the "pretty parts" and ignore its more complex dimensions.

Evolutionary biology can give us some clues about beauty in nature. A report on National Public Radio in 2004 revealed that "a desire and appreciation for beauty may...offer a competitive advantage in life."[4] The example in this report was of bowerbirds. It seems that female bowerbirds are attracted "by the decorations on a bower and the beauty of the male's mating display. Males that can perform elaborate displays are often the ones with well-developed genetic systems."[5] Other examples of nonhuman beauty abound: the plumage of various birds such as peacocks and cardinals; the bright colors of flowers, the deep aromatic scent of lilacs or lilies. And we also know that the blue of the sky and the green of trees and plants are particularly suited to our physiology. Although human behavior "is much more complex,...even something as purely beautiful as music may have helped people survive," a Penn State anthropologist suggests.[6]

The beauty of the cosmos has received attention as well in recent years. It ought to come as no surprise that scientists often turn to the language of beauty to describe what the universe discloses to us. Through the Internet, one can click on a link to a Web site that shows pictures taken by the Hubble telescope, which I can only describe as possessing breathtaking beauty.[7] Where does this beauty come from? Its complexity, its mixture of chaos and order, its literally awesome size, its drawing us into something *more*—all of these constitute beauty. Here, as with other beautiful realities, literal descriptions do little justice, but few would deny. the point that the universe is beautiful.

What we human beings call beauty may serve an evolutionary purpose for nonhuman life, but we are not (yet?) able to discern the kinds of aesthetic judgments that birds or insects make. I do not know whether the songs of birds are mostly to warn others of dangers nearby, as one report suggested in the summer of 2005,[8] or whether they are, perhaps, praising the beauty of our gardens. We can only speculate, or perhaps better yet, write poems about them. So what about human beings and beauty? It does seem that beauty is linked to human preferences, as a number of social scientists note. One recent study argues that beautiful people are more intelligent than less attractive people.[9] And another study that received a lot of attention in the spring of 2005 found that beautiful children were better protected by their parents in shopping carts than were less beautiful children.[10] This is not to say that a preference for beauty is hard-wired in human beings in a deterministic way, but it seems to play some kind of a role. And, of course, what is considered to be beautiful in one culture may not be so valued in another—although with increasing globalization, this may become less the case, as witness the example of the first African Miss World, Agbani Darego of Nigeria, who won in 2001 partly because she went against the African cultural mores that value a young woman's weight and size very differently than does the West.[11]

Is there anything natural about trying to be beautiful? Do we integrate beauty into human life, in our persons, and in our immediate environments because we are civilized? If we can grant that beauty has served—and still serves—some sort of evolutionary function, what does this mean for us as rational and moral human beings, who, while certainly attracted to beauty, also respond not only by instinct but also by rational and emotional reflection? We know that the face of the young child with a cleft palate says nothing about the way that the child responds to the world around her, especially if she is quite young and unaware of her deformity. But two examples of people who live with looks outside of the norm give us food for thought.

In one of her books, Annie Dillard writes poignantly about two young children—a girl and a boy—who both suffer from the condition of femoral hypoplasia—very short legs. About the younger of the two, a little girl, Dillard writes: "She has dark hair, bangs, and two wavy ponytails tied with yarn bows. Sure of her charm, she smiles directly at the camera; her young face shines with confidence and pleasure. Am I not cute? She is indeed cute. She is three." Dillard then writes of a five-year-old boy with the same condition: "He has a handsome young face, this boy; he stands naked against the black-and-white grid wall. He looks grim. He tilts his head down and looks up at the camera. His eyes accuse, his brows defy, his mouth mourns." Dillard says that at some point between the ages of three and five, "these kids catch on."[12] They come to see that they *will* be judged by their looks, that they *will* face stares and taunting, that their appearance *does* play a role in how they are perceived by others.

A second example: in her memoir about her friend Lucy Grealy, Ann Patchett recounts how

Lucy was convinced that no one would ever love her, that she would ultimately die alone, that she would never be happy. Lucy had had cancer of the jaw as a child, had endured chemo and radiation therapy, and had had multiple reconstructive surgeries, most of them unsuccessful. Patchett describes Lucy's face when they roomed together in graduate school:

> Her lower jaw had been a ledge falling off just below her cheekbone when we started college, making her face a sharp triangle, but now the lines were softer. She couldn't close her mouth all the way and her front teeth showed. Her jaw was irregular, as if one side had been collapsed by a brutal punch, and her neck was scarred and slightly twisted. She had a patch of paler skin running from ear to ear that had been grafted from her back and there were other bits of irregular patching and scars. But she also had lovely light eyes with damp dark lashes and a nose whose straightness implied aristocracy. Lucy had white Irish skin and dark blond hair and in the end that's what you saw, the things that didn't change: her eyes, the sweetness of her little ears.[13]

Lucy was also a talented writer, but she struggled all her short life—she died of a drug overdose in her thirties—with the complications of her looks. Would she have had the same struggles, insecurities, and addictions if she had not gone through what she did? We do not know. But we cannot really say that looks don't matter, especially when it comes to severe disfigurement. We read of doctors and nurses who go to poor countries and perform surgeries to correct cleft palates, of plastic surgeons who donate their time to repair disfiguring injuries on those who cannot afford the care, and, on a much more mundane level, of women who donate good used clothing so that poor women who cannot afford to buy them can have attractive clothes to wear to work, or prom dresses so that high school girls without the means to buy their own can have a pretty dress to wear.

Appearances *do* matter. We would consider it tragic if someone were unable to correct a disfigurement from birth or an accident, if a child with a correctable problem went without surgery because of lack of funds. Yet we—or at least I— find it problematic when a sixteen-year-old girl has breast augmentation surgery, when Hollywood stars have so much cosmetic surgery that their faces can no longer express any emotion, or when a slight young man has pectoral implants so that he can appear to be muscular. There is a line somewhere between the examples of the two children and Lucy Grealy and of those I just mentioned, when the importance of appearance for a decent life develops into an obsession with appearance that verges on, if not actually becomes, immoral. A few years ago at a high school reunion, my classmates and I gave one of our group a makeup, which consisted of a new haircut and new makeup. My classmate has a disabled child and was at the time in an unhappy marriage that was soon to end. I found the idea of our chipping in for a salon appointment to be a good deed, and indeed it was, as she emerged from the salon looking wonderful and happy. Not long after, she left her marriage, moved, and started a new life.

As I have reflected on these examples, it seems that *caring* for others' beauty and for our own is central. We wish for the other's good and happiness, a happiness that is *in some way* tied to our physicality, and we do what we can to promote this happiness. Yet, I do not think that the mother who spends $5,000 on her teenager's breast implants is necessarily really caring for her child. What makes the difference here? I suggest here—and return to it later—that a central dimension of genuine beauty is the quality of generosity. Real beauty both has and elicits generosity, and such generosity plays a central role in the Christian moral life.

No Good Models for Beauty

So there is beauty in nature, and we are somehow created with a desire for beauty, yet actively seeking beauty for one's person is seen negatively by many, especially those considering its moral connotations. This may be for good reason. Naomi Wolf has documented how the so-called beauty industry has worked to convince millions of women and men that they are not beautiful without artificially enhancing their natural looks and shapes.[14] Women are either too beautiful, in which case they are a threat, or they are not beautiful enough, and so they need to diet, exercise, and wear the right makeup and clothes so that they can be successful in life. Just this past year, Sheila Jeffreys has written a book entitled *Beauty and Misogyny*, in which she argues that the beauty industry imprisons women into practices that are not only demeaning but downright harmful.[15]

The issue of body image is one that I hardly need do more than mention. A widely cited study asked women what they would want most if they could have it, and the overwhelming answer was to lose weight, even if this meant a shorter life.[16] Television reality shows depict very ordinary-looking women in need of makeovers, some of them "extreme," and play on their (and perhaps our) convictions that their lives will be better if they have extensive plastic surgery, color and cut their hair, wear lots of makeup and buy lots of new clothes, and work out for months at a time with trainers. The medical literature describes the condition of "body dysmorphic disorder" to understand what goes on in the thinking of those with anorexia nervosa and bulimia.[17] There is more literature on this topic than I can even begin to mention, and it strikes most of us very close to home. A good friend of mine, having lost twenty-five pounds after going through a difficult divorce, wrote to me: "I hate to admit it but the main source of my depression wasn't work, kids, love, money but WEIGHT! Talk about being socialized. And the funny thing is that I looked humongous to myself; and yet nobody looks fat to me. Everybody looks great."[18]

If we look for religious statements about beauty, particularly as it is seen in women, we come up with a very interesting and troubling picture. Some of the early Christian fathers took a very dim view of women's beauty. For example, it is in Tertullian, a second-to-third-century Christian thinker, that we encounter one of the earliest Christian invectives against women's adornment. He writes:

[Woman should] affect meanness of appearance, walking about as Eve mourning and repentant, in order that by every garb of penitence she might the more fully expiate that which she derives from Eve—the ignominy, I mean, of the first sin.[19]

Tertullian goes on to say that ornamentation can be traced back to the fallen angels, and that God did not will the color purple—something that we might contrast with Alice Walker's character Shug, whose famous observation is that "I think it pisses God off if you walk by the color purple in a field somewhere and don't notice it."[20]

Jerome, a fourth-century patriarch, echoes Tertullian's ideas as he describes the young women of his time. I would just note that the Church fathers seemed to have a particular dislike for the color purple!

> When they go out they do their best to attract notice, and with nods and winks encourage troops of young fellows to follow them. Of each and all of these the prophet's words are true: "Thou hast a whore's forehead; thou refusest to be ashamed." Their robes have but a narrow purple stripe, it is true; and their head-dress is somewhat loose, so as to leave the hair free. From their shoulders flutters the lilac mantle which they call "maforte"; they have their feet in cheap slippers and their arms tucked up tight-fitting sleeves. Add to these marks of their profession an easy gait, and you have all the virginity that they possess.[21]

And we have only to look to Jerome if we want to find a religious reason for being thin:

> Let your companions be women pale and thin with fasting, and approved by their years and conduct; such as daily sing in their hearts: "Tell me where thou feedest thy flock, where thou makest it to rest at noon," and say, with true earnest-

17

ness, "I have a desire to depart and to be with Christ." Be subject to your parents, imitating the example of your spouse. Rarely go abroad, and if you wish to seek the aid of the martyrs seek it in your own chamber. For you will never need a pretext for going out if you always go out when there is need. Take food in moderation, and never overload your stomach. For many women, while temperate as regards wine, are intemperate in the use of food.[22]

The desert fathers also provide some interesting examples of statements regarding the beauty of women, although it seems that the most discerning abbesses and abbots observe that the real sin is in the heart of the monk, rather than in the woman herself. One of the sayings tells the story of the "certain solitary" who, one night, opened his door to find a woman standing there, pleading to be admitted. She, in fact, had bet some young men that she could seduce the monk. Rather than give in to his desires, the monk lit a candle and burned his fingers, one by one, "...and when it burnt and scorched he felt it not, for the flame of lust that was in him."[23] The woman, overcome by the piety of the monk, converted to Christianity on the spot. In the Middle Ages, women took rather seriously the idea that their beauty was an obstacle to their salvation. In a fascinating article, Jane Tibbetts Schulenberg writes of the "mutilated beauties" who deliberately disfigured themselves by cutting off their noses, or by deliberately scarring their faces so as to avoid rape or marriage.[24] The beauty of women is thus a hindrance to holiness.

The association of women with beauty, for good or ill, is not only a phenomenon of the past, but of the present as well. The theologian Hans Urs von Balthasar, whom I mentioned at the beginning of this lecture, provides an interesting if also troubling way of seeing the connection between women and beauty. For von Balthasar, the ultimate beauty of God is perceived by humanity in the form of Jesus Christ. This, I would say, is as it should be, because, from a Christian perspective, human beings come to God through Christ. Yet, when Balthasar describes the human response to God's beauty revealed in Christ, it is through the "Marian form"—that is, modeled on the Virgin Mary—that human beings are understood: ideally as feminine, receptive, obedient, virginal. Balthasar writes that the "feminine...is especially adapted to the sensory realm."[25] This is very much in line with his "nuptial vision" of the divine-human relationship, where the feminine is equated with the human, and where God is always the Bridegroom and never the Bride.[26] The feminine is always the beholder of true and divine beauty, always the receptive, waiting one. And even the beauty that is possessed by the feminine is always pure, spotless, and virginal.[27]

Such a portrait of beauty hardly corresponds with the experiences of real-life women or even, as Elizabeth Johnson would argue, with the lives of women in first-century Palestine.[28] The idea of feminine beauty in relation to the divine that emerges from Balthasar is that of the "Eternal Feminine," an idealized construct that places women on a pedestal and far above the gritty realities of life.[29]

These religious pictures of women's beauty—either as evil or as idealized—leave us without positive models to bring beauty realistically into our lives, to use beauty in such a way that it opens us up to the beauty of others and of the world itself. Is making oneself beautiful, or even making one's home beautiful, an immoral act? Or are they at best morally neutral? Does gender have anything to do with the moral lack of significance of personal and domestic beauty? Ought we to decry the waste of money, money spent on clothes, cosmetics, rugs, and even shower curtains, money that could have gone to the poor?

In my conclusion, I will comment on the hints we get from scripture here, including the one that I have just alluded to, but before that, I will draw on the ideas of two feminist writers who offer some helpful ideas on beauty. One is Iris Marion Young, in her essay "Women Recovering Our

Clothes,"[30] and the other is Heidi Epstein, in her book *Melting the Venusberg: A Feminist Theology of Music*.[31]

Beauty, Sensuality, and Order

In her fascinating and humorous essay, Iris Young talks about the pleasure that women get from clothes—imagining ourselves in soft wool, shopping together, touching beautiful fabrics. While aware of the feminist critique that charges the fashion industry with urging women to see themselves as men see them, to become an object for others' eyes by wearing the clothes that they are "supposed" to wear, Young suggests that there are other things at work here as well. She proposes that there are three things going on in women's fascination with clothes and shoes (a fascination I and many of my friends share as well). These are the pleasures of touch, of bonding, and of fantasy.

For her first point, Young draws on the ideas of French feminist thinker Luce Irigaray, who suggests that "feminine desire…moves through the medium of touch more than sight."[32] In a passage worth quoting, Young writes:

> Less concerned with identifying things, comparing them, measuring them in their relations to one another, touch immerses the subject in fluid continuity with the object, and for the touching subject the object touched reciprocates the touching,

21

blurring the border between self and other...
[Touch is] an orientation to sensuality as such
that includes all senses.[33]

Men's desire, Irigaray says, seems to operate more
through sight, and Young notes that sight is "dis-
tancing," as have a number of other observers.
We might consider here the connection with the
"male gaze" that art critics and historians have
described.[34]

Young's second insight is that "[c]lothes often
serve for women in this society as threads in the
bonds of sisterhood."[35] She describes women who
shop together as also exchanging intimacies and
knowledge of each other through the sharing of
experiences of trying things on, in suggesting to a
friend that something looks wonderful and is
worth the expense, or that this particular color
looks good on someone. In their shopping expeditions, women share with each other something of
themselves. Young writes of how women can shop
for hours and return home empty-handed, yet
thoroughly enjoy the experience, since they have
been able to delight in each other's company while
trying on beautiful clothes.

Third, Young suggests that women's relationship with clothes—which I am here including in
the female experience of beautifying one's person—"encourage[s] fantasies of transport and
transformation."[36] Young sees this as an exercise

in freedom, as she notes that "[o]ne of the privileges of femininity in rationalized instrumental culture is an aesthetic freedom, the freedom to play with shape and color on the body, to don various styles and looks, and through them exhibit and imagine unreal possibilities."[37] It is, quite simply, fun, to think about and try on clothes, to imagine ourselves in our beautiful new outfits, to play with the person we are and how we will be in these clothes. Just over ten years ago, I gave a plenary address at a national conference, and while the writing of my address occupied a large part of my time and energy in the months beforehand, I also searched carefully for the right dress to wear, and found one. The address went very well, and as I left the ballroom where I had given it, a colleague of mine at another university (and a previous Madeleva lecturer as well) came up to tell me how much she liked my lecture, and also how much she liked my dress. I would simply add to Young's observation that the fantasies of wearing just the right outfit are not mere fantasies, but help us to imagine ourselves confidently in the places we strive to go, like lecturing before hundreds of people in just the right outfit.

Heidi Epstein is a feminist musicologist, and in her development of a feminist theology of music she suggests that traditional musicology has understood music as an echo of the eternal harmony in heaven, reflecting the pristine order of the universe, especially as it is found in numbers and as established by God. Music has traditionally been seen to exemplify the "drive for order." When music most departs from its orderly and harmonic perfection, it becomes "feminine," chaotic, and its interruption by feminine chaos, fuzziness, and sensuality drives it away from its divine sources.[38] She notes how John of Salisbury remarks, "Let us sing vocally, but let us sing as Christians; let us sing sparingly but let us sing more in our hearts."[39]

Epstein argues that what is most often lost in these theories is the very embodiedness of music, the fact that we could not experience it at all if we were not embodied with lungs and throats to sing and blow, with arms and feet to play, with ears to hear. Yet, theologians like Augustine wrote of their struggles to hear the message behind the music, trying to be "…moved not by the song but by the things which are sung…."[40]

How are these ideas significant for our purposes? The roles of tactile pleasure, of personal connections, of alternative possibilities, of play and fluidity, of sensuality, and of wild extravagance are unexplored dimensions of beauty that more fully incorporate the body into our ideas of beauty. Traditional (male) ideas of religious beauty are spiritual ideas of beauty, and real physicality detracts from this beauty. Yet, there is no beauty without the body; beauty is always connected with its temporality and materiality. In the home and in a good relationship with one's own person, a love for beauty includes the joy of tactility and connecting, an appreciation of fantasy and the extravagance of the way nature operates, an overflowing generosity toward oneself and toward one's family and friends. Real beauty is embodied, involves the senses, facilitates connections, and, in nature, overflows with excess.

Young's and Epstein's ideas suggest an alternative model of beauty: one not defined by either the lack of women's full, sensual, and sometimes voluptuous bodies or by idealized bodies that exist nowhere in reality, but a beauty solidly grounded in our sensual experiences, a beauty that is not primarily heavenly but rather quite earthly. The beauty of women in relation to our persons and our homes is a beauty that is sensual, that connects, that is extravagant and overflows, and that is not carefully measured in perfect harmony. To love ourselves, then, is to love the finite (fluid, rounded, soft) realities that we are, not the false ideals (clear, pristine, untouched) that we can never imitate.

Beauty and Generous Self-Love

"Love your neighbor as yourself" is one of the "two great commandments,"[41] yet there has been a strong theme in the Christian tradition that self-love is potentially something very dangerous. One of the earliest challenges to traditional Christian understandings of love, sin, and grace was Valerie Saiving's essay in the *Journal of Religion* in 1960, when she suggested that the root of sinfulness in human beings might not be, as Reinhold Niebuhr suggested, in too much pride and self-love, a too-large ego and self-centeredness, but rather in its opposite: that women too often had a lack of self-love and, too often, put others before themselves. Since then, many others have picked up on this theme, and it has become one of the most well-developed ideas in feminist theology.[42]

The significance of self-love has not been a theme only for feminists; a number of Christian theologians have developed it in recent years.[43] This emphasis on self-love has accompanied an emphasis on *mutuality*, a theme that has also been taken up by many thinkers, both those who would identify themselves primarily as feminists and those who would not.[44] It is worth noting that Thomas Aquinas argued strongly against loving one's neighbor more than oneself.[45] I would like to pick up on the themes that have been developed by feminist theologians surrounding love of self and mutuality and suggest a connection with beauty and generosity.

In order to do this, I turn to the ideas of Elaine Scarry, as she has developed them in her book *On Beauty and Being Just,* and those of some other recent writers on beauty.[46] In her book, Scarry develops a theory of beauty and identifies some key features of beauty. These are, first, that beauty is sacred; second, that beauty is unprecedented; third, that beauty is lifesaving; and fourth, that beauty incites deliberation.[47] She summarizes these features at one point by remarking: "Something beautiful fills the mind and yet invites the search for something beyond itself, something larger or something of the same scale with which it needs to be brought into relation."[48]

Similar ideas are developed by other writers on the topic of beauty. Frederick Turner, in his book *Beauty: The Value of Values*, mentions the sense of recognition that accompanies a sense of beauty, and its inexhaustibility and depth.[49] He also comments that "[b]eauty can almost be *defined* as an absence of the desire for power, possession, success, political victory in themselves" and continues by noting that "...there is a 'giving-away' in beauty, a sense of nothing to lose...."[50] David Bentley Hart includes beauty's objectivity, its ability to cross boundaries, and its freedom.[51] All of these authors point to a certain fluidity in beauty, while it is, at the same time, quite particular.

A very loose and preliminary definition of beauty would be that of a kind of ordering of material, intentional or not (as in nature), in a way that presents a unique vision or sensory experience of some dimension of the experienced world that gives the beholder both pleasure and a sense of deeper meaning.[52] I would emphasize my qualified use of such terms as *ordering* and *vision*. By order I do not mean to refer to some idea of hierarchical order (although this may be involved), but to something more along the lines of an arrangement that is somehow pleasing. And by vision, I do not intend to indicate only visual beauty and to exclude music or tactile beauty, but rather to refer to the completeness of the presentation as it is experienced by the beholder.

The authors I have mentioned here, and many others, describe an excess that is characteristic of beauty: what is truly beautiful cannot be put into a careful formula, nor can it be adequately described. And beyond beauty's inexpressibility is what Scarry describes as beauty's quality of "greeting": "At the moment one comes into the presence of something beautiful, it greets you."[53]

There is, I suggest, an intrinsic *generosity* that is characteristic of beauty. Real beauty does not exclude; rather, it invites. Real beauty does not "count up," but rather flings its gifts to anyone who asks. Real beauty invites exploration and depth; it does not shut the door prematurely to the questioner. Beauty is always ready to give more. When we encounter a beautiful work of art, we find ourselves unable to exhaust fully the beauty that it offers. When does one get tired of great works of art, of sunrises and sunsets, of gardens, of our loved one?

Such generosity is one of the main ways in which Jesus describes God: as the father of the prodigal son who welcomes him back without condition and throws a huge party; the vineyard owner who pays everyone a full day's wage, even those who only worked an hour or two; the God whose love is so immense that this God is with us in our very flesh. Much of what has been traditionally taught in Christian ethics has emphasized the radicality of God's love and how we should emulate it: we should turn the other cheek, forgive seventy-seven times, give the stranger all our clothes when only our cloak was requested. Such love is incredibly generous and often quite difficult, and so it is quite often. But what often emerges from this picture is a life of hardship, a life where we turn to the other with a sense of obligation and gritted teeth, a stripped-down life as if true Christian love required us to give up everything that was fun or beautiful. Christian justice, this image suggests, is hard and radical.

I would like to suggest a different way of looking at this generosity: it is indeed radical. Yes, the extravagant love for God and of God is one that *will* inevitably lead to the cross, but the cross is not the final answer. If real beauty is physical, sensual, embodied, and overflowing, it will eventually die, and so much a part of beauty is our realization that it is so fleeting. We want to capture beauty, so we take touristy pictures, buy books, have plastic surgery, but in doing so we only try to put beauty in a box and refuse to let it be.

But our love of others and ourselves cannot be easily put in a box or a formula. The ability to appreciate beauty comes from a generous heart; indeed, beauty itself enlarges the heart. The sense of beauty from which I suggest we learn is akin to nature's beauty and generosity where there is always enough. To be generous with one's own beauty means to welcome others to one's self. If we can agree—as I think we can—that there is an intrinsic generosity in beauty, an openness, an invitation, then a theology of beauty that is incarnate and grows from our sense of beauty in the natural world is also a theology of generosity: to oneself and to others.

It seems to me that our contemporary images of beauty are far from generous to the self. As my friend commented about herself, everyone else looked fine, but she felt herself to be huge. Consider how our ideals of beauty are ideals of stinginess, of self-mortification, of deprivation. Consider how we talk of being good as we limit our diets, swear off chocolate or ice cream, and exercise ourselves to exhaustion. Now I am not suggesting that there is not a problem with obesity in our country and in developed nations, or that we should feel free to go on shopping expeditions whenever we feel an emptiness inside, or that we should be able to buy $600 shower curtains. What I am saying is that we have lost an ability to live generously with beauty. When we fail to acknowledge and appreciate beauty—our own, another's, nature's—we are failing to give glory to God. We are failing to love our neighbor as our self.

Later I will attempt to retrieve a Christian feminist understanding of humility, which, I will argue, in the long run coexists with self-love and generosity. But for now, let us all consider how we can be more generous with ourselves and others, how we can appreciate beauty in all its forms, and how we can notice beauty in the color purple and in the many other places where it beckons to us.

II

WOMEN, BEAUTY,
AND THE CHURCH

Last summer, one of the graduate students whose dissertation I had directed gave me a thank-you gift after she had formally received her PhD. It was a large book called *Churches* and included photographs of numerous places of worship around the world—some of them famous, and some less well-known. All of these churches were quite beautiful, from the soaring arches of the Gothic cathedrals to the spareness and simplicity of contemporary chapels.

I have a particular fondness for the beauty of churches. I remember well one experience of walking into a Gothic cathedral. It was my first trip to Europe, and I was in Paris. I had planned a day trip to see Notre Dame of Chartres, the famous cathedral written about by so many. I had been to a cathedral in Brussels and found it impressive but not overwhelming, and I was very much looking forward to being overwhelmed by Chartres. Before my trip to Chartres, I visited the cathedral of

Notre Dame on the Île de la Cité, expecting to be impressed but not awed—I was saving that for Chartres. But as I walked into the cathedral that day, to my complete surprise, tears came to my eyes as I saw the rose window and the beautiful light that filled the massive space. I remember standing there for some time, simply dumbstruck. I expect that the builders of Notre Dame would have been pleased at my reaction, of being awed by its beauty. When I went to Chartres the next day, I was again duly awed, but not as surprised as I was when I entered Notre Dame.

Churches are meant to be places of beauty, to stir the mind and especially the heart to God. And their beauty strikes women and men alike. Particularly in Catholicism, beauty plays an important role in worship, unlike some contemporary evangelical churches where there are few, if any, symbols or art work,[54] Catholic worship is meant to appeal to the senses as well as to the spirit: the colorful vestments of the priest and the matching altar cloths, flowers, music, the smell of incense (when it is used), statuary, the architecture. As Don Saliers puts it,

> Aesthetic experience as such is not the primary aim of the public worship of God. The praise, the glorification of God, and the transformation toward the Holy is. Yet such glorification and sanctification require human modes of communi-

cation, and must "touch down" into the whole range of human experience....If the primary intention of liturgical celebration is participation in the mystery of God's holiness and the divine self-communication, then the beautiful is always at the service of the holy.[55]

I believe that Saliers is right: in worship, the beautiful *is* at the service of the holy. Going to church is different from going to a concert. (I try to remember this when I sit next to someone who cannot sing in tune!) But I also believe that this means we must choose our symbolism very carefully. If God truly is truth, goodness, and beauty, then our symbolism ought to reflect this. And when it comes to symbolism related to women, the tradition seems to suggest that women cannot symbolize the beauty of God in worship.

The presence of women in Christian churches has a long and complex history, in part because of concerns about the proximity of the presence of women to the presence of God. I suggest that this is tied to concerns about the beauty of women conflicting with the beauty of God. Women's beauty ties human beings to the earth, to (usually male) desires, to the many things that hold us to the earth when our eyes, we are taught, ought to be watching heaven. Women's beauty is a secular beauty, even a profane beauty, whereas God's beauty is spiritual. The beauty of the Virgin Mary is the one exception to this, but remember that Mary is both virgin and mother.

Before Vatican II, it was expected that women were to cover their heads in church, and I am old enough to remember wearing a folded piece of Kleenex bobby-pinned on my head when I forgot my mantilla. There were certain places in churches, like the altar, where women couldn't go when there was a Mass—although women could be there to clean and dust when the church was not being used for worship. Girls could not be altar servers, something that annoyed me as a child when I could recite the Latin just as well as, if not better than, my brothers. Yet I was also aware that in some way, even though I was not allowed into the sacred spaces, this was my church as well. This complex and ambiguous sense of being both included and excluded is a familiar feeling to many worshiping women.

In this section, I will explore the ways in which women's physical presence, their dress, and their voices have been seen to be threats to the spirituality and beauty of Christian worship. I will then turn to the ways in which women have contributed to the beauty of churches, through their handiwork, their dress, and their voices. Finally, I will explore the ways in which women have made and found places of worship outside official church spaces and have maintained a physical and sensuous beauty that refuses to be spiritualized.

Such a sense of beauty calls us to reconsider the ways in which we think about God and beauty.

"No Women Allowed"

In her fascinating book *A History of Women in Christian Worship*,[56] Susan J. White describes her experience of visiting an ancient cathedral in Macedonia. Knowing that women and men were separated from each other in worship, she went into the narthex, where the women would have stood while the liturgy was going on, so that she could have a feel for what worship was like for them. She expected to feel angry and excluded, but as she looked around the narthex, she became aware of large frescoes of female figures covering the walls and ceiling. She writes:

> Suddenly, I knew something about women's experience of worship that I had not known before: I understood that when women gathered to pray in this place, surrounded by the presence and prayers of the great cloud of women witnesses to the faith from the past, it was an experience of solidarity and empowerment rather than an experience of segregation and repression.[57]

I mention this story for the same reason that White begins her book with it: although women were, and in many cases still are, excluded from sacred spaces in worship, we ought not to jump to negative conclusions too quickly. White's book itself shows why the history of women and worship is not "the shortest book ever written," as one of her friends commented as she was writing it, but rather a rich and complex story. And as Sandra Schneiders wrote a number of years ago, there is a "flip side" to women's experiences of exclusion and marginalization.[58] Nevertheless, it is instructive to note how carefully women's physical presence or absence in the presence of the holy has been regulated by Canon Law.

Let me give you a few examples. The 1917 Code of Canon Law held that "in harmony with ancient Church order, the women in Church [should] be separated from the men."[59] Although this was not the case in practice in many, probably most, churches, the rule was there. Women were also not to distribute holy communion, not to be altar servers, not to be readers, and were to have their heads veiled. One of the more interesting regulations held that "sacred linens must first be washed by men, before women touch them."[60] Although I have not been able to track down the exact part of the Code, I have read a number of references to one canon that forbade women to ride in the front seat of a car with a priest. Now these canons make no reference at all to beauty; at their core remains what I would describe as a strong though unarticulated sense of concern for ritual purity. But I would argue that this regulation against women's presence, voice, or even their handling altar linens is also a fear of men being distracted, or, at worst, seduced, by the physical presence of women, which would then prevent men from being in the presence of God. Women's physical presence and their beauty detracts from or even obscures the beauty of God.

Since the revision of the Code in 1983, these regulations may seem somewhat quaint to modern ears. Surely women's presence is no longer a problem in churches, and even I, for one, would suggest that both women *and* men consider a little more carefully how they dress for church. (Being my mother's daughter, I still cannot wear jeans to church.) Yet, there remain a number of practices and regulations that concern women's physical presence. For example, in the new Code of Canon Law only men can be formally installed as acolytes (altar servers) and lectors (readers). Women can be "temporarily deputized" to fulfill the functions of these roles, but cannot formally assume them, as can men.[61] Women can also and indeed do serve as eucharistic ministers, but they do so in an "extraordinary" capacity—that is, when the "ordinary" minister cannot, for some reason.[62] Basically, women serve in these capacities as a "last resort." When the late Pope John Paul II visited Chicago in the fall of 1979, I had considered going to the Mass in Grant Park, since popes don't come to Chicago every day. Yet, when I heard that only men would be allowed to be eucharistic ministers, I decided that I would not go, and instead I met with my women's group, where we celebrated in our own way.

Now it might be argued that I am making too much of these examples. Women serve formally in many capacities in the church today, including those of diocesan chancellor, marriage tribunal judge, parish council member, as well as the more familiar ones of pastoral coordinator, pastoral associate, and, of course, as Director of Religious Education, particularly of small children. Ministry at the altar is not a right, but a privilege; no one has a right to ministry, as the Vatican is careful to say. Yet, I am concerned with the picture, so to speak, that is presented of what worship ought to look like.

I still occasionally come across a question to an expert (usually a priest) as to why women are distributing communion when there are priests available. The liturgical expert will usually say that, despite local practice, the Canon Law holds that women can distribute communion "in emergencies, whenever any other suitable person cannot be found."[63] This is true too in cases of emergency baptism. The one exception to the rule of women not being sacramental ministers is, of course, in marriage, where the couple are the ministers to each other and the priest or deacon is there as a witness for the church.

But let us consider the picture of worship that develops. I think of the elaborate funeral of Pope

39

John Paul II, with the cardinals and all the clergy robed spectacularly in beautiful colors, while the nuns wore black and white. There were, to be sure, a few instances of blue, worn most often by African nuns. A friend of mine who was in Rome at the time commented on how she had seen the windows of a store displaying multicolored vestments for various liturgical feasts, clothing all designed for male clergy. Habits for women religious were, of course, black.

Liturgical worship is meant to draw the mind and heart to God, so let us just digest this point: in ideal circumstances, as Canon Law would require, when one's eye is on the altar, there are no women in the picture. We are so accustomed to this that the presence of women in liturgical roles is for some problematic, as we shall see.

Let me turn now to my second, somewhat brief, point, which concerns how women are to be dressed for church. As I commented previously, before Vatican II girls and women were to have their heads covered in church. While one would be hard put to see this in practice in most churches today, there is no lack of interest on Web sites in the issue of women wearing veils. A number of sites mention quite positively the hierarchical order in which women are to submit to men, while others note that women's immodesty in dress makes them less attractive to devout men as potential wives. It is interesting to note the revival of interest in women wearing veils among conservatives. One woman writes: "Clothing is never without meaning, and a man intuitively understands that the veil represents a gentle submission that lies at the very essence of womanhood and femininity."[64]

This particular quotation is of interest because of the vision of the beautiful woman that emerges. And if a woman dares to wear clerical dress, such as an alb, we are warned of the dangerous potential of such practices. The Web site for the conservative Catholic women's organization Women for Faith and Family not surprisingly comments, "[t]he symbolism of women wearing clerical vestments and performing liturgical roles traditionally reserved to ordained priests is very strong, and should not be ignored."[65]

In the present, women pretty much wear whatever they want to church, at least if one can judge by the attire of the girls and women in the places where I have attended. And, as I noted before, while both women and men ought to give more thought to what they put on for church, this freedom of dress is a very recent phenomenon. A little later I will comment on the wearing of hats in the African American religious community. But suffice it to say that in the long history of the church, a great deal of ink has been spilled over proper attire for worship, particularly for women, as we noted in Tertullian's and Jerome's comments cited earlier.

Not so long ago, women were not to wear anything sleeveless, particularly in European churches, and in pictures of papal audiences, I always find it interesting to see the wife of a world leader, or sometimes even a woman world leader herself, Catholic or not, wearing a dark black mantilla. It is, we are told, a sign of respect.

In Islam, the question of whether or not to wear the *hijab* is not only a personal issue but a political one as well, as the French government has forbidden Muslim women students to wear it to state schools. Some of my Muslim students at Loyola have spoken quite frankly about the consequences of wearing *hijab*. One student decided to wear it as a sign of her religious faith, but found herself constantly being asked questions about it and being stared at. She decided not to wear it anymore, since the anonymity that the *hijab* is supposed to confer on the woman turned into its opposite. Another student began wearing it when the month of Ramadan began, and when I asked her about it, she said that she and a friend of hers had together decided to begin wearing it as a sign of their devotion. Another Muslim student confessed to me that she wore the *hijab* because her brothers insisted on it, and she sometimes came to class (Women and Religion) without it. I cannot begin to address the issue adequately here, but I would just note that one purpose of the *hijab* is to dress in such a way that the woman will not be a distraction to men. In

March of 2005, a Muslim woman scholar, Amina Wadud, led a prayer service attended by both men and women, which violated Muslim tradition. The reaction among many in the Muslim community was so negative that she had to conduct her classes by video conferencing from home, because the school was concerned about danger both to her and to her students.[66] What does this say about women in the presence of God?

A third, and brief, point has to do with women's voices. Many of us are familiar with the phenomenon of the *castrato*—the man with a beautiful voice who was castrated as a child so as to maintain his high voice. In the late sixteenth century, and into the late nineteenth, there were choirs of *castrati* who took the soprano and alto parts of music. This was done so as not to hear the voices of women in church. I also came across a reference to an Anglican church choir in Scotland that now welcomes women as full members. This choir's Web site notes that in the past, a few women may have sung with the men and boys' choir; however, they did not process with the choir, as was the tradition, but were concealed in the choir stalls.[67] The point, of course, is that boys were preferable to women in church choirs. Women's voices lack the purity of boys' voices, and the presence of women would distract the other choir members, the clergy, and the congregation (presumably male).

As I have already noted, traditionally women have been excluded from the office of lector, but can, in special circumstances, read the scriptures. This too is a practice that is not observed in many places; I serve as a reader at my own church, and the person in charge of instructing readers is a woman. Nevertheless, women are, again, the choice of last resort. And when it comes to preaching, if women do preach at a Eucharist, their efforts are not to be called "preaching," but rather "offering reflections," and, according to church regulations, these reflections are not to be offered after the proclamation of the Gospel, but at the end of the eucharistic liturgy.[68] I am grateful that at my own church, our woman pastoral associate preaches occasionally, and when she does so, it is immediately following the Gospel. Yet, every time she does this, someone in the congregation complains to the archdiocese that church rules are not being followed. My colleague and friend Mary Catherine Hilkert has already graced the Madeleva lecture series with her reflections on the authority of women's voices.[69]

Women's Handiwork and the Beauty of Churches

My mother was a needle worker, and our house is graced with many of her pieces: a framed sampler on our stairway, a little cross-stitched child's prayer in our bedroom ("Now I Lay Me Down to Sleep") that she worked on when she was pregnant with me, a needlepointed footstool, a quilt, quilted Christmas ornaments, table linens, and needlepointed Santa coasters. She hated to have her hands idle. My nieces and nephews who were born before she died all have afghans and sweaters she knitted for them, and there are sweaters, scarves, hats, and mittens that I still wear, many of which she made with leftover yarn. She made quilts for the nursing home where my stepfather spent his last years, and they were raffled off each year. She even needlepointed a little door hanging for a friend of mine who admired mine (hers says "Janet is sleeping"). We have a little needlepointed hanging that says "damper open" on one side and "damper closed" on another. One of the most humorous projects she undertook was to knit uteruses, so that my sister, a nurse who taught childbirth classes to expectant parents, could demonstrate how the uterus stretched during pregnancy and opened up for the baby's head. My mother loved to recount how she would answer when someone politely asked her what she was knitting. She taught my sisters and me how to knit and do needlepoint and I think of my mother whenever I pick up knitting needles or a needlepoint canvas.

My mother, I think, is part of a very long historical sorority of needleworking women who worked canvases and tapestries not just to keep their hands busy, but also for the glory of God. Consider the elaborate embroidery done on vestments and altar cloths, the needlepointed kneelers in so many Anglican churches, the embroidered tapestries that covered the walls of churches and that also helped keep the spaces warm or cool, as well as the baptismal gowns worn by generations of babies. Like the architects of the great cathedrals, the creative minds and hands that produced these are anonymous, but I think we can assume that many of them were women. I can hardly imagine a church without artwork, or a Mass without vestments. But women were and are involved in more than embroidery or needlework.

Women were and still are also involved in maintaining the altar linens, Church regulations to the contrary. They care for and polish the patens, chalices, and ciboria; make sure that appropriate flowers are ready for liturgy; repair altar cloths and vestments; decorate the church for feasts; and embroider, as my mother did, baptismal bibs for christenings. In my research for this lecture, I found many Web sites for altar societies both in the United States and around the world. And while I confess that on occasion in the past I may have thought of altar societies as "women's work," while I was doing the "heavy lifting" as a theologian, I found myself deeply touched by reading about the histories of altar societies and the good work that they continue to do. I also felt great sadness as I read of societies that no longer have any younger members and so, as one put it, face "a very bleak future."

Let me just quote from the material about one altar society at a church in Kentucky, to give you an idea of its activities:

The society is responsible for many things such as—caring for altar linens, candles, incense censer, baptismal font, vacuum cleaners, etc. The Society also makes all christening bibs for the babies being christened. They also have purchased vestments for the priest and altar boys. They have also had the Chalice and Ciborium gold plated, and contributed funds for the purchase of new furniture in the Sanctuary. They have contributed funds for the building of the gym and the rectory, and purchased a bus, which was used by the students attending St. Paul's and St. Scholastica's Schools in Covington. Counting the money for the church collections, church weekly cleaning, cleaning the holy water fonts, and taking care of cleaning and replacing candles are some of the society's other duties. They also decorate the church for holidays including the Christmas and Easter season. Presenting gifts to O.C.I.A. candidates and participating in the program, hosting elderly at the Vacation Bible School, preparing and serving at Catholic High school graduation and confirmation class celebrations, working at various money making projects are some additional ways the Society participates in church community functions. Until recently the Rosary Altar Society supplied all of the hosts for Holy Communion in our church. The society prepares and conducts other miscellaneous affairs as needed. The society's main fund raiser is selling their famous strawberry cakes and other items during the annual Strawberry Festival.[70]

Now, from one perspective, one could dismiss these tasks as demeaning women's work, a way to keep the elderly ladies of the parish busy. Yet, consider the work that is being done and consider the fact that all of this is necessary work. Like maintaining a home, these are tasks that simply need to be done, yet are considered to be the liturgical equivalent of "housework," something that most of us would rather not do ourselves, and hire out if we can. Yet without this work, churches, like houses, would not be clean or inviting, and would utterly lack beauty. Beauty, as we are so often told by the beauty industry, requires a great deal of work, and some of this work is far from glamorous. I want to raise up the work of these countless anonymous women who have helped to maintain the beauty of our churches. Without them, we would not be able to behold this beauty as well as we have.

A second example of how women have worked to make the church a place of beauty can be found in the tradition of African American women's church hats. This is a fascinating and inspiring example of how the traditional Pauline injunction that women should worship with their heads covered has been transformed into a way for women to feed their hunger for beauty and for self-respect. For many of these women who spent their days working in blue- or pink-collar jobs, or who had to wear uniforms as domestic servants, Sunday was a day to wear their best clothes and to adorn their heads with stunning hats. The book *Crowns: Portraits of Black Women in Church Hats* is an anthology of pictures of African American women wearing their Sunday best, and it has been made into a play by the noted playwright Regina Taylor. It was performed at the Goodman Theater in Chicago during the 2003–2004 season.

The one who wore a hat well had "hattitude." She had pride in herself, a love for beauty, and a desire to wear her best in the presence of the Lord. One woman pictured in the book comments: "I think that [putting on your best] grows out of the African American tradition that says that when you present yourself before God, who is excellent and holy and most high, there should be excellence in all things, including your appearance. It's a holdover from African traditions, the idea of adorning oneself for worship."[71] Another says, "As a little girl, I'd admire women at church with beautiful hats. They looked like beautiful dolls, like they just stepped out of a magazine. But I also knew how hard they worked all week. Sometimes, under those hats, there's a lot of joy and a lot of sorrow."[72]

I confess that I love hats and own a couple that I have few chances to wear, mostly at summer weddings. I did not inherit this from my mother, who had, as she used to say, the wrong face and head for a hat, but she loved the fact that I could wear them well. Wearing hats, like the tradition of the altar society, is, for a number of reasons, no longer widely practiced, even in the African American community. Most women welcomed the relaxing of the requirement that our heads be covered, and I do not know a single woman my age or younger who is involved in an altar society or who has special hats for church. I suspect that these traditions will soon be quaint reminders of the past. Yet, I think it is worth considering what these practices tell us. In both cases, women were either barred by men from sacred spaces and given menial work to do, or they had a rule imposed on them by men—both were so that women would not intrude on the sacred beauty of the church. But in both cases, women from all ends of the social and economic spectrum turned these situations into opportunities for beautifying their worship spaces. I doubt that the women who have been active in altar societies or who have proudly worn their plumed and feathered hats to church considered themselves oppressed, and I do not think that we should consider them in this way either. Their concern, I suggest, was the one that I earlier quoted from Don Saliers: that their sanctification "touched down" into their experience.

So when we walk into a beautiful church, with clean windows that allow the stained-glass light to filter in, with pews that are free from dust and clutter, with tapestries or artwork that draw our hearts heavenward, with women crowned with elaborate millinery, we should be grateful for the work that women have done to maintain this beauty, and for the love of self and of neighbor that moves them to share their love of beauty with the whole church. These examples reveal a true love of God, self, and neighbor, and a deep generosity of spirit that sees beauty as a precious gift of God that must be shared. And while I deplore the demeaning attitudes that have prompted exclusion and sexist requirements for women's exclusion, at the same time I celebrate the creativity with which centuries of women have turned these prohibitions into occasions of beauty and grace.

Other Altars

Women of my generation will surely remember the grade-school processions, May crownings, and home altars that were a central part of the pre–Vatican II Catholic girl's experience. I remember borrowing my mother's dresser linen—those cloth doilies made for the tops of dressers to protect them from marks—and setting up on my desk or dresser a statue of Mary with juice glasses for vases of lilies of the valley, and blue cloth draped around the mirror or bulletin board. It was a chance, I think, to exercise the kind of creativity we saw on our church altars, both the one in the middle but especially the ones on the side. Beauty and holiness were not meant only for church, but also for the home, and even for the bedroom of a nine-year-old girl.

In her memoir *Chasing Grace*, Martha Manning writes of her women's group that meets monthly and serves for her as a kind of church. She notes: "Women have rarely known primacy in temples or churches, and so we continue to find it at *other* altars, with our sisters, who have *never* lacked for words, only for voices and volume."[73] The last thirty years or so have seen an explosion in rituals designed by and for women; Manning's experience is hardly uncommon. My point here will not be to give any sort of history of these groups, because such work is widely available.[74] Rather, I want to highlight the dimensions of these practices that are oriented toward enhancing an appreciation for the beauty of the earth and of women, and linking this beauty with a concern for justice.

It is instructive to note that in the accounts of women's ritual and liturgy I am familiar with, there is virtually no explicit mention of beauty. But it is there nevertheless, intrinsically, in the ways in which the material of worship is described. In her book *Ritualizing Women,* Lesley Northup lists the emerging patterns in women's worship, which include the uses of ritual images and spaces, many of them connected with women's domestic lives. Images include the circle, horizontality, nature, the body, childbearing and mothering, and women's crafts.[75] In Northup's analysis, the term beauty is never mentioned. But I would argue that the "raising up" of what is ordinarily seen as secular, worldly, or simply ordinary, as a medium of revelation of the sacred, is an implicit recognition of its inherent beauty.

In her brief book *Feminist Liturgy: A Matter of Justice,* Janet Walton is a bit more explicit in her references to beauty and the arts.[76] She writes that the use of song, movement, space, and images are all central to successful liturgy. She notes as well that sometimes adjustments need to be made to familiar texts for the sake of justice. But while these adjustments are made for the sake of inclusivity, in the long run I would argue that they contribute to the greater beauty of the liturgical experience.

I have argued elsewhere that there is an implicit concern for beauty and justice in the work of feminist theology.[77] In her now classic book *She Who Is,* Elizabeth Johnson repeatedly makes the point that "the symbol of God *functions.*"[78] In a section worth quoting at length, Johnson writes:

> In the church [the] exclusion [of women] has been effective virtually everywhere: in ecclesial creeds, doctrines, prayers, theological systems, liturgical worship, patterns of spirituality, visions of mission, church order, leadership and discipline. It has been stunningly effective in speech about God....Upon examination it becomes clear that this exclusive speech about God serves in manifold ways to support an imaginative and structural world that excludes or subordinates women. Wittingly or not, it undermines women's human dignity as equally created in the image of God.[79]

No one who has read Johnson's work could take issue with the aesthetic quality of her prose, and indeed, her book has inspired both visual works of art as well as a book of prayers.[80] But even if one is to set aside Johnson's own beautifully crafted prose, the point remains that liturgical language and symbols—poetry and prose and works of art—have the power to inspire as well as to deaden. Feminist theology's effort has been precisely to home in on the ways in which our "imaginative and structural world" has been a constricted one—indeed, a profoundly unjust one, where women's beauty has been seen as unfit for the place of worship.

Beauty vs. Justice?

Do adjustments such as the ones that Walton mentions necessarily detract from the beauty of worship? In an editorial for the journal *First Things,* Richard John Neuhaus, a former Lutheran pastor and now a Roman Catholic priest, commented about the news in 1997 that a committee of U.S. Bishops was given permission by Rome to use "moderately inclusive horizontal language."[81] *Horizontal* language refers to language about human beings, while *vertical* language refers to language about God. Neuhaus interestingly observes that inclusive vertical language is "heretical."[82] He argues that there is, in fact, no demand for gender-inclusive language and he further asserts that efforts on the part of the U.S. Catholic Bishops to make liturgical language more inclusive are a way to "successfully rebuff...zealots here who pressed for more radical changes..."[83] Neuhaus approvingly quotes Cardinal Christoph Schönborn, who argues that "language is not an arbitrary vestment that you can take or leave,"[84] like fashion, and suggests that making changes in liturgical language will conflict with the beauty of the liturgy. Neuhaus is concerned with the aesthetic quality of liturgical language, yet nowhere does he give an example of how "moderately inclusive horizontal language" is aesthetically or theologically deficient. In the conclusion of his editorial, he again quotes Cardinal Schönborn, who writes:

> Beauty is one way to God. It should never be separated from goodness and truth. Beauty without goodness is not beauty; so love for the poor has to be cultivated together with love for beauty—and, of course, with love for truth.[85]

I find it to be both sad and sinful that a sensitivity to the power of language to shape our thinking is considered to be "zealotry," and that linking beauty with goodness and truth can be done at the same time one dismisses concerns for gender justice. Moreover, both Schönborn and Neuhaus ignore the fluid and changing quality of language itself. Neuhaus observes that "[t]here was a time when converts to Catholicism were suspected of succumbing to aestheticism, which is worshiping the holiness of beauty. No more."[86] But for Neuhaus, and others, to equate a concern for a more adequate language—not to mention more adequate symbols or even music—with philistinism is to miss the point. It is precisely *because* of the power of language and symbols to shape our imaginations that feminists have argued for greater attention to them, as have African Americans before them. Beauty and justice do not have to compete for primacy, as Cardinal Schönborn correctly observes. It is possible to have both.

As a musician and one who is also concerned with the aesthetic dimension of liturgy, I can agree in part with Neuhaus's concerns for beauty in the liturgy. I, for one, find the exclusive use of soft-rock music written since Vatican II for eucharistic liturgies in most U.S. Catholic churches to be tiresome and even at times offensive.[87] Granted, some of the hymns from the first half of the twentieth century and earlier are well forgotten, and granted as well that some of the more recent hymns are aesthetically quite powerful. Moreover, one ought to note that Catholics have not been, for the most part, well disposed to congregational singing, as most Protestants have, and that contemporary music might have a stronger appeal to young people. Nevertheless, it is possible to combine creatively music from many time periods, including the present, in a way that serves both spirituality and musicality. I have seen this done in a few churches where Gregorian and Taizé chant, contemporary Christian soft-rock, African American spirituals, and traditional hymns coexist harmoniously. The solution is to use the best examples of music of different genres in appropriate places in liturgy. And in my own experience, young people are quite open to a variety of musical styles, and many find the music of the pre–Vatican II church to be an exciting discovery. I have twice taught a course in Theology and Music and my students have responded eagerly to the music of Hildegard of Bingen, Palestrina, and Bach with the question, "Why haven't we ever heard this beautiful music before?"

But liturgy is not only about aesthetics. I continue to attend my church, much as I dislike most of the music we sing, because of the quality of the homilies, the sense of community that I experience, and the ways in which I am both nourished and challenged spiritually and theologically. Inclusive language in liturgy is not a problem because of its aesthetic quality, or lack thereof, *pace* Neuhaus et al., but rather because it challenges some basic assumptions that have gone unquestioned for centuries: that God can be spoken of only in male terms; that our language adequately reflects the structures of our society, church, and imaginations; and that the beauty of God would be marred by zealous inclusive language and imagery.

Feminist liturgists' efforts have been to widen our vision and sense of beauty: in hearing how the language of God our Mother can inspire new forms of prayer, in seeing how the image of a woman presider can affect women and men in ways they had never before imagined, in using symbols and gestures that spark new ways of realizing God's presence in our midst. Real beauty causes us to see or sense something more, something beyond the immediate. When liturgy is tied to an exclusive picture of God, then it is no longer beautiful. And by the same token, when a liturgical celebration is motivated purely by pragmatic concerns, it has lost a sense of beauty as well. It is somewhat ironic to note that there was, in fact, considerably more liturgical freedom in the pre–Vatican II days than there is now in that the eucharistic liturgy was one among many liturgical and sacramental practices. Processions, home altars, rosaries, novenas, all were additional ways in which the lay person could participate in worship creatively. For good reason the Eucharist was named the "summit and source" of the Christian life by Vatican II, but this focus has had the effect of placing nearly all liturgical energy and emotion into one hour on Sundays.[88] It should not surprise us that so much controversy surrounds the practice of the Eucharist, as bishops exclude politicians for their voting records; as gay men, lesbians, and their supporters wear rainbow sashes to Mass to protest the church's teaching; as women drift away from church, tired of repressing their anger.

Surely women's senses of beauty have influenced our worship spaces for thousands of years, yet church tradition has been that women's own beauty is best left at the church door. So it is one of my concerns that my words here may invite us to reconsider the beauty of our churches and our worship. Can we truly "give glory to God" while excluding half the population from imaging this glory? Are aesthetic concerns for the beauty of language violated when we expand our language—and therefore our imaginations—to include women? I think not, and the work of beauty that women have been doing for so many years is witness to the many ways, both small and large, in which women's work has been "for the greater glory of God."

III

WOMEN, BEAUTY, AND JUSTICE IN THE WORLD

Women's connections with their own beauty and their contributions to the beauty of churches may not initially seem to be appropriate subjects for theological aesthetics, as I suggest they are. They have rather been the subject matter for beauty, fashion, and craft magazines. Few would deny their aesthetic qualities, however, even if these qualities have been either commercialized or trivialized. But when it comes to the wider world, it would seem that these more intimate connections with beauty might be inadequate. Such is the place for great architecture, for city planners, for arts funding for public education.

Yet women's art and craft, as I will show, can serve to connect beauty and justice in illuminating ways. I will draw on some examples of women and beauty in Africa to suggest that their ways of combining beauty, practicality, and concern for the community can inspire us to make these connections in our own worlds and with them as well.

The Lessons of African Women's Art and Craft

In the summer of 2002, I was part of a small group of Loyola faculty and staff who traveled to East Africa on an immersion trip. We visited a university, orphanages and schools, and women's cooperatives and training centers, and also encountered the magnificent natural beauty of Africa in places such as Lake Nakuru, where we saw thousands upon thousands of flamingoes; the Masai Mara, where we had some rather uncomfortably close encounters with baboons and elephants; and Mount Kilimanjaro, which we saw rising majestically from the Tanzanian savannah. Yet, even with all of this spectacular beauty, one of the most memorable places we visited was the tiny village of Lwak, near Kisumu in western Kenya, on the shores of Lake Victoria. Lwak is a desperately poor place, and the people there struggle to survive amid the crisis of HIV/AIDS, the effects of governmental corruption, and the vagaries of the weather. Shortly before we arrived in June, most of their tomato crops had been washed away by torrential rains.

While we were there, we were also gifted with the hospitality of the women of Lwak. After we had spent the better part of a day touring the fields, visiting the village where the cooperative store sold soaps and preserves, and driving along muddy, rutted "roads" to see some of the cooperative projects—including a newly hand-dug well—the women of the village threw us a party. They brought their couches and chairs outside and covered them with lace doilies, and they served us food that they must have spent days cooking. There was a small band of men musicians, and although we visitors were all exhausted, we ate and danced and sang with our generous hosts into the evening. I was struck then as now by these women who beautified themselves, their homes, and their village in honor of their guests. The women who belonged to the cooperative wore matching dresses that they had sewn by hand and their homes had pictures on the walls and flowers in their tiny gardens. The woman who hosted the party had buried her husband a few months before, after he had died of AIDS, and she herself was HIV positive. Somehow, though, her love for beauty had survived, as had her generous sense of hospitality and her commitment to her village.

In the nearly four years since I visited Africa, I have felt myself drawn to learn more about its people, its land, its struggles, and its beauty. As the magazine *National Geographic* described in its September 2005 issue, Africa is much more than it may seem to the West. What I have learned from the women of Africa are lessons in beauty and justice that extend from their families to their communities and, ultimately, to the world. In this last section, I will describe the work and contributions of a handful of African women. I will then reflect on what they have to teach me—a white, privileged, highly educated, middle-class American woman—and perhaps some of the rest of us. For many of the women of Africa, beauty and justice go hand in hand.

One of the best known African women today is the 2004 Nobel Peace Prize winner, Wangari Maathai. Some of you may recall the announcement when the prize went to the first African woman ever to be so honored. In the summer of 2005, Wangari Maathai visited my church in Evanston as part of her visit to the Chicago area, and I heard her speak about her life and her work. She was a compelling speaker, and the church was filled to overflowing as we heard her talk about her efforts in reforestation and with women's groups. The words of the Nobel committee described her contributions this way:

> Peace on earth depends on our ability to secure our living environment. Maathai stands at the front of the fight to promote ecologically viable social, economic and cultural development in Kenya and in Africa. She has taken a holistic approach to sustainable development that embraces democracy, human rights, and women's rights in particular. She thinks globally and acts locally.[89]

It is not immediately evident that either Wangari Maathai or the Nobel Prize committee thought of her work in the language of beauty and justice. I would guess that they did not. But her work shows evidence that beauty is at least an implicit, if not an explicit, dimension of it. My own thesis is that historically, and for the vast majority in the present, women have seldom taken the time, or, for that matter, have had the time, to theorize about beauty. Beauty for women is, rather, tied closely to the way one lives and acts. It is interwoven into women's lives and is much less an ornament than a central thread: a practice, and not simply an idea.

The Nobel citation recounts Maathai's efforts in the 1980s to block the construction of a sixty-two-story skyscraper in Uhuru Park in the center of Nairobi. I have been to Uhuru Park and was struck by the vast expanse of green and trees in the middle of one of the largest cities in Africa. Maathai was successful in her efforts and the plans for the skyscraper were abandoned. Her efforts continued as she has worked to preserve the environment in Kenya, where 90 percent of the forests were lost between 1950 and 2000.[90] And for her efforts, Maathai was imprisoned a number of times under the former President of Kenya, Daniel arap Moi. Because women are the major food producers in Africa, and firewood is the major source of fuel, these efforts have been

Herculean, as she has succeeded in "combin[ing] science, commitment, active politics, and faith in God."[91] Her goal is "to protect God's creation 'so that this earth can be the Garden of Eden that God created.'"[92]

Not only has Maathai worked to preserve the forests, but she has also worked to connect the issues of poverty and women's education with justice, as the Nobel citation pointed out. The Nobel committee observed that ecological issues are at the heart of much of the conflict in the world today, not only in Africa, but in South America, the Philippines, and other places as well. As I write these words in the fall of 2005, the media are filled with the images of the aftereffects of hurricanes Katrina and Rita, where decades of inattention to the pleas of ecologically minded citizens and municipalities have finally borne their bitter fruit. And in Louisiana, Mississippi, and Texas, it is the poor, and especially women and children, who have suffered the most.

When we consider the beauty of the earth, we think of the great forests, mountains, and oceans. But this beauty is not just ornamental; it is not a theory; it is not merely decorative. This beauty serves a fundamental purpose: the continued survival and flourishing of the earth and all who live on it. When the beauty of the earth is damaged or destroyed, we all pay for it eventually, but poor women, men, and children inevitably pay first, as we see in the example of the desertification of sub-Saharan Africa. This is true not only in Kenya, but also in Somalia and especially Darfur. The integrity of our earth is indeed beautiful, but it is functional as well. It is impossible to have one without the other. To choose between beauty and justice is a lose-lose situation; one may perhaps initially gain something, but there is inevitably loss in the long run.

Let me give another example of the relationship between beauty and justice provided by some other women of Africa. After I returned from my trip to Africa, I was on the lookout for things that related particularly to African women. In the fall of 2002, I was on a plane to New York for a conference and happened to flip through the in-flight magazine. There was a very small sidebar that described an exhibit in New York City, an exhibit that unfortunately I would have no time to see, but I jotted down the information. Eventually I tracked down some books by the photographer whose work was the focus of the exhibit. Margaret Courtney-Clarke has spent decades photographing the work of African women, from the Berber women of Morocco to the Ndbele women of South Africa, whose artistic work is not only stunningly beautiful but also practical and of service to the community.[93]

Courtney-Clarke's first book describes the house painting and beadwork of the Ndbele women of South Africa. For generations, these women have painted murals on their homes in bright colors and designs and have also worked beads into intricate patterns to be worn. These practices have survived years of civil war and apartheid, and, sadly, they are no longer as widely practiced as they once were. Globalization, modernization, urbanization, and other forces too complex to name mean that fewer younger women are learning these skills. The house paintings involve complex geometric patterns in distinct designs. Some of them have, in recent years, begun to incorporate features of modern life, such as cars, planes, and electric lights, in their murals, but they are transformed and adapted into Ndbele culture. Beads are also a significant part of Ndbele life. Children wear beads before they wear clothing, and initiation ceremonies for both boys and girls involve wearing beadwork especially designed for these rituals of passage.

It would be both inappropriate and presumptuous of me to say what the meaning of these practices is. Anthropologists themselves are not unanimous in their own judgments. But for this particular Western observer, the incorporation of the house painting practices into the lives of the Ndbele people raised for me the issue of beauty and its role in everyday life. The Ndbele people have endured apartheid, forced relocation, civil war, and worse, and yet, these women continue to paint their houses as expressions of the craft they learned from their mothers and, I think, as a way of keeping their daily lives not only functioning but also beautiful. House painting is not something these women do to "while away the time." It is, rather, a part of their culture, a means of both self- and communal expression.

Maya Angelou has written the text for a children's book about Ndbele culture entitled *My Painted House, My Friendly Chicken, and Me.*[94] The narrator of the book, a young Ndbele girl, says,

> I don't know why, but Ndbele people do not call anything beautiful. They will say that the best thing is good. All Ndbele women paint their houses, and I want you to know, stranger-friend, no one's house is as good as my mother's. She has started to teach me to paint good, very good designs.[95]

In another one of her books about African women—Berber women from Algeria, Morocco, and Tunisia—Courtney-Clarke again documents the craft of women, this time in weaving and pottery.[96] In her introduction, she describes her search for these women's work and the reactions of the Berber men when she asked about it: "The Berber men had no concept of what I was in search of and thus could not comprehend my passionate interest in their wives' seasonal domestic activities."[97] It has been the men's work in pottery and jewelry that has achieved renown, not the women's. Moreover, the work of the women, as is true of much of the work of non-Western cultures, is under assault from the same processes I described above.

Courtney-Clarke was drawn to their work for the same reason she has been documenting the work of other African women: it is stunningly beautiful and it witnesses to the creativity and strength of a group of people otherwise hidden from the rest of the world. One can hardly page through her books without a sense of reverence and awe. And it is worth mentioning as well the enormous burdens that women shoulder in these societies: of raising families and food, of drawing water and tending crops, of maintaining life under the most difficult of circumstances.

Yet another example of African women's crafts appeared as a story in a Chicago newspaper in the spring of 2003.[98] This article documented how Tutsi and Hutu women, many of them widowed after the brutal civil war in Rwanda in the early 1990s, had begun to come together to weave baskets. These baskets had formerly been used as engagement or wedding gifts, but they were now available for sale. The women found that working together to weave these baskets also had the effect of reconciliation and helped to heal their pain.

Women whose husbands and sons had been murdering each other years before found solace and strength in their joint endeavor of basket making. The money from the proceeds of the sale of the baskets is used for the women and children.

It is not my point here to romanticize the women of Africa. To be sure, increasing modernization has brought good as well as ill to these people. Courtney-Clarke is aware that many of the women who are so skilled at these crafts lack formal education; just finding them was a challenge, because many women do not ordinarily go out in public. In her book on Berber women, Courtney-Clarke quotes the elderly matriarch of a Berber family on what she would want for her daughter if she were to give birth today. She responded, "I'd send her to school...I would like her to be a doctor."[99]

The very practical concern of this woman for her children is a clue to what these women's work suggests about the relation of beauty to justice. There is creativity, practicality, and a concern for the wider community in their work. Each woman has her own patterns, her own individual stamp on her work. Yet, this creativity is tied in with practicality as well. These works are distinctive, and each points to its own designer and maker. These are houses meant to shelter families from the elements; they are pots that carry water; cloaks that cover the body from the harsh sun; baskets that hold food. There is no sharp divide between creativity and practicality; they work together. Although some of these works may indeed end up on the walls of museums or in the homes of the wealthy, they are there obviously out of their context and use.

As much as, if not more than, their creativity and practicality, these are works that make sense only within their community. They are not individual works of art, with no precedent, unique unto themselves. Each house is very much like the next, although it is also different. Baskets and pots resemble each other, although each has the stamp of its maker. They are interwoven into the community's life. The skills are passed down from mother to daughter. And as we have seen, even the term *beauty* does not quite capture these objects. They are good: pleasing to the eye, yet also functional. Might we say they also embody the truth of the lives of these women? Might we say that they are examples of the unity of goodness, truth, and beauty?

Beauty, Humility, and Justice

One of the points that is emphasized by many writers on the topic of beauty and justice is the way in which beauty "de-centers" the self. Elaine Scarry writes, "At the moment we see something beautiful, we undergo a radical decentering."[100]

We cease to be the center of attention for ourselves, as perhaps we usually are; we become aware that our own vision is expanded through the beautiful thing we encounter. Other writers comment on the humility that is involved in the encounter with the beautiful.[101] We no longer loom as large as we might have in the world of beauty. We see ourselves as smaller, less significant, as beauty grows. But this growing smaller is in fact not a diminution, but in reality an expansion of our vision and of our world.

Such a decentering, I believe, is appropriate when considering the ways in which women's artistic and craft work has affected their own lives and the lives of those who encounter them. Women's art work also offers something of a model for the unity of beauty and justice, particularly as it moves beyond a focus on the individual to the larger community. Yet, to suggest an attitude of decentering and, even more, of humility, is to raise a red flag, particularly for feminist ethics.

In the thirty or more years that feminist theologians have attended to issues in ethics, one of the main themes has been the challenge to traditional understandings of sin, grace, and virtue. As we have already seen, Valerie Saiving asked whether the traditional ways in which theologians such as Reinhold Niebuhr and Paul Tillich identified sin— as arrogance, egoism, overassertion of the self— was as applicable to women as it was to men.[102]

She asked, was it true that women needed to become more selfless? Was it not the case that women were already socialized into putting others first, in their failure to develop themselves fully? Perhaps women's sin was more focused on a lack of self-development, a tendency to diffuse the self, to give the self away too readily, rather than the tendency to overassert the self. Since Saiving first published her work, this theme has become one of the most prominent ones in feminist theology. Feminist theologians such as Judith Plaskow, Susan Nelson, Barbara Hilkert Andolsen, and others have further developed this theme as they have worked to redefine the theology of sin and grace from a more critical and informed feminist perspective.[103] Such work has overflowed into new areas such as violence against women and children, the long-term effects of abuse on children, and the way in which Christian theology understands the role of self-sacrificial love.[104]

So when the ideas of humility and of a decentering of the self arise in relation to beauty and ethics, it is not surprising that concerns about the traditional theological privileging of humility and self-sacrifice are raised. Does this privileging not play back into the traps for women that such theologies have presented? I would like to suggest here that attending to women's practical experiences of beauty offers some hints at a possible retrieval of the role of decentering and humility.

This retrieval will be especially attentive to the ways in which self-sacrificial virtues have been distorted and have worked against women and their own personal development. Yet, to reject entirely the need for a certain amount of decentering, and even a role for humility, is to rule out the possibility of an ethics oriented toward the community as well as the self. The primacy that feminist ethics has placed on the *relational* character of human being as well as our autonomy offers some helpful directions, as Margaret Farley has argued.[105] But I want to push this issue a bit further by arguing that it is only by de-centering ourselves that we are able both to see beauty and to share it, to make our world *both* beautiful and just. Without such a decentering, we run the risk of elevating beauty above truth and goodness, making it a private and personal goal and failing to share it with others. When this happens, beauty becomes a possession, something bought and sold. It is no longer shared; it is, rather, owned. And it is no longer good. Yet, such a decentering of self and retrieval of humility can only come about when they are joined with self-love and generosity, to one's self as well as others.

There are certain dimensions of the appreciation of beauty that writers on this subject emphasize, quite justifiably. Philosophers and theologians have stressed certain habits and attitudes. These include attentiveness, particularly attentiveness to detail, a heightened awareness, a sense of reverence, and the obligation to behold and enjoy.[106] Particularly in relation to the world of nature, ecological ethicists emphasize the fact that natural beauty cannot be commodified. The beauty of the natural world is fragile and interdependent and cannot be separated from the processes that maintain that beauty.

Yet, it seems that those of us who live relatively comfortably in the developed world live in a world where beauty is often up for sale. Not only can one pay to get one's wrinkles, age spots, and cellulite removed, it is also possible to decorate one's home in the style of Martha Stewart, Ralph Lauren, Calvin Klein, or any number of other famous designers by shopping at discount stores. It seems that almost every week there is a new television show about home design, and I confess that I enjoy watching some of these shows. In some interesting ways, at least some of the virtues listed above can be applied to the world of home design: attentiveness to detail—anyone who has ever watched Martha Stewart make a holiday decoration can only be amazed by the details she includes; a heightened awareness—how many of us, after having watched a television show or read a decorating magazine now look at a piece of furniture or a wall color only to see it as tired, passé, and in desperate need of change; even the obligation to behold and enjoy can be exercised with the purchase of a few magazines or fabric samples, or by window-shopping at the local mall. Yet, I doubt that a sense of reverence, of a decentering of the self, of a turn to others, are most characteristic of how we feel when we have finished a decorating project. It seems to me that perhaps some of us may well be in need of a little decentering, a little humility about the relation between beauty and justice. A comparison between the women of Africa and the women of the home decorating shows can be sobering and decentering as well. Perhaps such a decentering—the kind that we experience when we behold the art and craft work of these women—might help in engaging us more intensely in the struggles for justice, especially justice for women, in the world.

The kind of retrieval of humility that I have in mind is one that centers on our awareness of our place in our own world and in the universe. This kind of humility means that we are aware of the needs of others, not so much as needs that precede our own—as is unfortunately the case for many women in the world whose custom is always to feed the menfolk first, children second, and then to eat what is left—but as needs that may have as much priority as our own. The particular kind of humility that we feel as we encounter something beautiful is not in any way degrading, but rather uplifting. We are in awe of the handiwork of the artist, or of the magnificence of nature; we see our smallness and feel its greatness. I think it is this sense of humility that is most missing in much of the developed world today, when we can see beauty any time we wish, when beauty is something we can buy, if we have the money. My reflections on the women of Africa and their attentiveness to beauty and practicality is one way of reminding ourselves that we can encounter beauty in the most unexpected places, and that such beauty can help to transform our relationship with others and with the natural world. It also suggests that the fleeting "beauty" that we buy at the cosmetic counter or discount outlet lacks goodness and truth.

As always, it is helpful to consult the experts when considering traditional virtues like humility. And although I may have some qualifications to add to what Thomas Aquinas has to say about humility, in the main his ideas are quite instructive. Aquinas notes that humility is a virtue ordered to a "difficult good," that is, a good that has both positive and negative qualities to it.[107] He has in mind the point that there is both a movement toward a good while at the same time there is also a restraint; this is the case with humility, when we desire the good yet must moderate our desires at the same time. Thomas sees humility in relation to what he calls the "appetite": that is, it appeals primarily to our desires, rather than to our reason. And although Thomas sees humility as a virtue ordered primarily to God and not to others, I would suggest that we in the so-called developed world might consider the virtue of humility as a civic, in addition to a personal, virtue, as humility is so that "a man ought not to ascribe to himself more than is competent to him according to the position in which God has placed him."[108] Humility is an appropriate valuing of one's gifts in relation to others,[109] and includes a "moderation of spirit."[110]

I suggest that the particular humility that theoreticians of beauty have described and the virtue of humility that Thomas describes have something in common: a thoughtful sense of one's place in the world and before God. And this sense of place applies as well to our attitude toward the natural world. Yet, I make these remarks about humility with a deep sense of humility on my own part, because such virtues, I believe, are not appropriate for all. One of the great contributions of feminist and liberation theologies has been to highlight the "social location" of the theologian, and it is quite clear that the virtue of humility has been distorted and misused, particularly toward the already humble and vulnerable, who have been encouraged and even commanded to humble themselves even more intensely before others and God. Thomas Aquinas himself notes that "due moderation must be observed in the outward acts of humility."[111] But this virtue is particularly appropriate for the comfortable and the powerful and, so I suggest, for those of us in the comfortable and powerful West. It is, indeed, a virtue I wish our national leaders would consider working on for themselves and for the nation as a whole.

Yet, I want to emphasize that this virtue does not exist alone. As Thomas Aquinas noted, humility comes after the three theological virtues (faith, hope, and charity, with charity being the highest), after the intellectual virtues (understanding, science, wisdom, art, and prudence),[112] and, finally, after justice.[113] My suggestion is that humility accompanies a generous love of self and of others, as I developed earlier in the first section. Without an appropriate sense of humility, it is impossible to set aside one's own concerns on behalf of the more pressing needs of others. Yet, a distorted sense of humility might mean that one neglects one's needs in favor of others, who may in fact be less needful. An appropriate experience of humility can be the result of an encounter with the beauty of the earth, and the beauty of works of art in all their variety. Its result is generosity.

Such humility causes us to pause, to enjoy, to take in the details, and to consider how this vision of reality reorients our vision of the world. In the art of the African women I have described, we encounter a combination of beauty and practicality, and this combination challenges us to envision ways in which we might combine these as well.

Modern categories of beauty as a pure and impossible ideal, as "spiritual," as perfection, fall short of the very finite, earthy, and particular baskets, bowls, and houses. This encounter with beauty suggests a rethinking of our traditional categories of what constitutes the good, the true, and the beautiful.

Another helpful expert to consult in relation to beauty, justice, and humility is one of the great "founding mothers" of Christian feminist ethics, Beverly Wildung Harrison. In a lecture that she gave to a group of Protestant laywomen entitled "Doing Christian Ethics," Harrison outlined the basic task of Christian ethics, one that I think can help to underscore the potential contributions of thinking about beauty in relation to our moral lives. Harrison defines the task of ethics as involving "two things—to improve our ability to reflect on and also to choose better or worse ways of shaping our personal or social actions."[114] Ethics, she stresses, is not simply a task for the professional; in fact, we all do ethics, every day, by the kinds of decisions we make and the lives that we lead. Harrison emphasizes that the task of ethics is for everyone, not just academics or religious leaders. In her remarks, she underscores the point that for Christians,

> invoking the principle of "love" is not the revolutionary note in Jesus' moral teaching. It is, rather,

81

the critical criterion he offers—that our love be aimed at those who have suffered exploitation and injustice—that sharpens and specifies the direction of our efforts. The transformative force of the Christian ethic, what the ancient prophets called hospitality to the stranger, defines the most urgent strangers as those who are currently the most excluded ones.[115]

Harrison also argues that "in [her] ethical approach, our identities always begin with 'We,' since we are relational beings, rooted in inescapably social lives."[116] Such a relational attitude involves a sense of one's place in relation to others, which is, at its core, what the virtue of humility is all about. Harrison's outline of Christian ethics can help to sort out the ways in which attention to the lives and work of women, especially the ones in most urgent need, can offer clues to a feminist theological aesthetics that is both appreciative of beauty—indeed, even humble before it—and also learns from it a more adequate way to consider the relation of individuals, the community, and the world.

Although theological aesthetics as it has been done in mainstream theology has emphasized the glory of God and the human attitude of reverence before and obedience to God's glory, my suggestion is that a feminist theological aesthetics and ethics are done "from the ground up," and are rooted in careful attention to the ways in which women's artistic and craft work weaves together creativity, practicality, and community. Such attention involves an awareness of the source of this work and the means for creating it; its place in the lives of women, men, and children; and its role in maintaining the lives of not only individuals, but their communities as well. To engage in a decentering process and even to act humbly before the beauty of the work of art or craft is to participate in a dialogue, where one can learn from the artist and the work, where we allow the work of art to speak to us and to direct our attention to dimensions of the world that we may have never seen. Thus careful attention to the details of women's work in Africa involves placing the work within the context of their lives, and understanding the nature of the efforts that go into it. Rather than insisting on a detachment from practical ends, we can see in their work how practicality and beauty can work together.

Women, Sacramentality, and Justice

As I have written elsewhere, "feminist theology shares with the Christian tradition a reverence for the earth and for the body...all of creation is potentially revelatory of God and has intrinsic worth, not just that worth bestowed by humans."[117] In the previous section of these reflections, I have emphasized the ways in which women's works of art and craft are indeed sacramental: they are ways of encountering the beauty of God in both expected and unexpected places. Like the sacraments, they are not purely individual creations, but rather are connected to wider communities: the family, the local community, the world. Yet, there is a sense in which the sensual dimension of human experiencing and knowing still carries a hint of the old dualisms. For example, in the *Summa Theologiae,* Thomas Aquinas writes:

> It follows, therefore, that through the institution of the sacraments, man, consistently with his nature, is instructed through sensible things; he is humbled, through confessing that he is subject to corporal things, seeing that he receives assistance through them; and he is even preserved from bodily hurt, by the healthy exercise of the sacraments.[118]

Although having to be "instructed through sensible things" may be, for Aquinas, a humbling experience, one can also consider the benefits of our corporeality, as does the music theorist Victor Zuckerkandl, who writes:

> A God enthroned beyond time in timeless eternity would have to renounce music....Are we to suppose that we mortals, in possessing such a wonder as music, are more privileged than God? Rather,

to save music for God, we shall hold, with the Greeks, that God cannot go beyond time. Otherwise, what would God do with all the choiring angels?[119]

Indeed, what would God do with them? But we know that in fact, God so loved the world that God became one of us, and in the process, made the earth and all who live upon it to be the place where we encounter God.

My own love of music dates back to my childhood when I would listen to my mother play the piano and, occasionally, accompany herself singing one of her favorite songs. She encouraged my love for music, making sure that I had piano lessons as a child and tickets to the symphony as a teenager. We would sometimes play four-hand music together, and when she listened to me practice, she could always identify the mistakes, but would also sing along with the pieces she knew. Shortly before her death, she was pleased to give me a gift of money that allowed me to buy a new piano, and a little less than three years ago, my husband and I put on an addition to our house so we could accommodate a grand piano, again thanks to her. When I play the piano, I feel a connection with my mother and a connection to all the beauty of the world as well.

As Thomas remarks above, we are instructed "through sensible things," and so we are instructed not only intellectually, but also morally and aesthetically. Following from this sacramental principle, our moral imaginations need this kind of attention as well. Iris Murdoch reminds us of the ways in which great art can be instructive: "It is important too that great art teaches us how real things can be looked at and loved without being seized and used, without being appropriated into the greedy organism of the self."[120] It is not only great art that can teach us this, but it is also the many ways in which women have encountered and created beauty. We can, to be sure, be "greedy organisms," yet we can also come to be generous with ourselves and with others so that we can appreciate the many dimensions of beauty in ourselves, in others, and in the world, and to nurture that beauty into its full blossoming.

I have suggested in these pages that having to choose between goodness and beauty is a false dichotomy, much like the false dichotomies that have plagued our tradition for millennia: spirit and body, male and female, reason and emotion, light and dark. And although women have found themselves so often on the lesser side of the dualism, they have also refused to accept this situation.

It seems appropriate to close these pages with the words of a song written on behalf of women workers, words that suggest the bread that not only fills us materially, but also spiritually.[121] The song also brings to mind the work that women have done for so long on behalf of themselves as well as of men and children:

> As we go marching, marching, in the beauty of
> the day,
> A million darkened kitchens, a thousand mill
> lofts gray,
> Are touched with all the radiance that a sudden
> sun discloses,
> For the people hear us singing, Bread and Roses!
> Bread and Roses!
>
> As we go marching, marching, we battle too
> for men,
> For they are women's children, and we mother
> them again.
> Our lives shall not be sweated from birth until
> life closes;
> Hearts starve as well as bodies; give us bread, but
> give us roses.
>
> As we go marching, marching, unnumbered
> women dead
> Go crying through our singing their ancient call
> for bread.
> Small art and love and beauty their drudging
> spirits knew.
> Yes, it is bread we fight for, but we fight for
> roses too.
> As we go marching, marching, we bring the
> greater days,

the rising of the women means the rising of
    the race.
No more the drudge and idler, ten that toil where
    one reposes,
But a sharing of life's glories: Bread and Roses,
    bread and roses.

Our lives shall not be sweated from birth until
    life closes;
hearts starve as well as bodies; bread and roses,
    bread and roses.

NOTES

1. Michelle Gonzalez is one exception to this, although she does not see his hostility to feminism as much of a concern as do some others, including myself. See her article "Hans Urs von Balthasar and Contemporary Feminist Theology," *Theological Studies* 65/3 (September 2004), 566–95.

2. I am thinking here particularly of the work of von Balthasar. See his multivolume works, *The Glory of the Lord: A Theological Aesthetics*, 7 vols. (Edinburgh: T & T Clark, 1982–1990), and the *Theological Dramatics: Theological Dramatic Theory*, trans. Graham Harrison (San Francisco: Ignatius Press, 1988).

3. "Men buying more beauty products; industry begins catering to image-conscious males," http://www.newstarget.com/005132.html.

My thanks to my graduate assistant, Jesse Perillo, for his hard work in tracking down many references, and to my husband, William P. George, for his love and support.

4. National Public Radio Report, "In Evolution, a Taste for Beauty Has a Purpose," October 4, 2004; http://www.npr.org/templates/story/story.php?storyId=4057069.

5. Ibid.

6. Ibid.

7. See http://hubblesite.org/.

8. See Luis F. Baptista and Robin A. Keistar, "Why Birdsong is Sometimes Like Music," *Perspectives in Biology and Medicine,* 48/3 (Summer 2005), 426–43.

9. See Adran Furnham, "Insight," *Telegraph,* September 16, 2004.

10. "Are Unattractive Kids Loved Less?" http://www.uofaweb.ualberta.ca/prl/news.cfm?story=35170.

11. Agbani Darego was crowned Miss World in 2001.

12. Annie Dillard, *For the Time Being* (New York: Vintage Books, 1999), 65–66.

13. Ann Patchett, *Truth and Beauty: A Friendship* (New York: HarperCollins, 2004), 11–12.

14. Naomi Wolf, *The Beauty Myth: How Images of Beauty Are Used Against Women* (New York: William Morrow, 1991).

15. See Wolf, *The Beauty Myth,* and Sheila Jeffreys, *Beauty and Misogyny: Harmful Cultural Practices in the West* (London: Routledge, 2005).

16. "Many students would trade shorter life

for ideal weight," http://www.californiawineand-food. com/news/weight-poll.htm.

17. See J. Kevin Thompson, *Exacting Beauty: Theory, Assessment and Treatment of Body Image Disturbance* (Washington, DC: American Psychological Association, 2004).

18. Personal communication, July 27, 2005.

19. Tertullian, "On the Apparel of Women," in *Ante-Nicene Fathers*, Vol. 4 ed. Alexander Roberts, DD, James Donaldson, LLD, and A. Cleveland Coxe, DD (Peabody, MA: Hendrickson Publishers, 1994), Book I, Chap. I, p. 14. Tertullian's ironic comments on God and the color purple are found in Chap. X.

20. Alice Walker, *The Color Purple* (New York: Washington Square Press, 1982), 178.

21. Jerome, "Letter to Eustochium" (Letter XXII), in *Ante-Nicene Fathers* III:27, same editors, 1st quote is p. 27; 2nd is p. 28.

22. Ibid., III:28.

23. *The Desert Fathers*, ed. Helen Waddell (Ann Arbor, MI: University of Michigan Press, 1972), 79–80. The story of the abbess chiding the monk for his noticing that the one he encountered was a woman appears on p. 73.

24. Jane Tibbetts Schulenberg, "The Heroics of Virginity: Brides of Christ and Sacrificial Mutilation," in *Women in the Middle Ages and Renaissance: Literary and Historical Perspectives*,

ed. Mary Beth Rose (Syracuse, NY: University of Syracuse Press), 29–72.

25. Aidan Nichols, *The Word Has Been Abroad: A Guide through Balthasar's Aesthetics* (Edinbugh: T & T Clark, 1998), 33, quoting from *The Glory of the Lord.*

26. See my "Can God Be a Bride?" *America,* November 1, 2004.

27. See, for example, von Balthasar's reflections on the femininity of Mary and the church in *The von Balthasar Reader,* ed. Medard Kehl and Werner Löser, trans. Robert J. Daly and Fred Lawrence (New York: Crossroad, 1982), 231–34.

28. Elizabeth A. Johnson, *Truly Our Sister: A Theology of Mary in the Communion of Saints* (New York: Continuum, 2003), esp. chap. 9 "Women: The Socio-Cultural World," 185–206.

29. See Johnson's critique of von Balthasar and others in *Truly Our Sister,* 57–60.

30. Iris Marion Young, "Women Recovering Our Clothes," in idem, *Female Body Experience: "Throwing Like a Girl" and Other Essays* (Oxford and New York: Oxford University Press, 2005), 63–74.

31. Heidi Epstein, *Melting the Venusberg: A Feminist Theology of Music* (New York: Continuum, 2004).

32. Young, "Women Recovering Our Clothes," 69.

33. Ibid.

34. Laura Mulvey, "Visual Pleasure and Narrative Cinema," *Screen*, 16/3 (Autumn 1975), 6–18.

35. Young, "Women Recovering Our Clothes," 70.

36. Ibid., 71.

37. Ibid., 74.

38. Epstein, chap. 1, "Phallic Rage for Order: Traditional Theologies of Music," in *Melting the Venusberg*, 11–31.

39. Ibid., 16.

40. Ibid., 19.

41. Matthew 22:39.

42. This point has become almost a given in feminist theology. Valerie Saiving, "Human Experience: A Feminine View," *Journal of Religion* 40 (1960); for two representative examples, see Judith Plaskow, *Sex, Sin, and Grace: Women's Experience and the Theologies of Reinhold Niebuhr and Paul Tillich* (Washington, DC: University Press of America, 1980); Barbara Hilkert Andolsen, "Agape in Feminist Ethics," in *Feminist Theological Ethics: A Reader*, ed. Lois K. Daly (Louisville, KY: Westminster John Knox Press, 1994), 146–59.

43. See, for example, Edward C. Vacek, *Love, Human and Divine: The Heart of Christian Ethics* (Washington, DC: Georgetown University Press, 1994); Stephen Pope, *The Evolution of Altruism and the Ordering of Love* (Washington, DC: Georgetown University Press, 1994); Bernard V.

Brady, *Christian Love* (Washington, DC: Georgetown University Press, 2003).

44. See, for example, *Embodied Love: Sensuality and Relationship as Feminist Values,* ed. Paula M. Cooey, Sharon A. Farmer, and Mary Ellen Ross (San Francisco: HarperSanFrancisco, 1987); Margaret Farley, *Personal Commitments: Beginning, Keeping, Changing* (San Francisco: HarperSanFrancisco, 1986), as well as the books mentioned in n. 42 above.

45. Thomas Aquinas, *Summa Theologiae* II–II, q. 26, a. 4: "...a man ought, out of charity, to love himself more than he loves any other person."

46. Elaine Scarry, *On Beauty and Being Just* (Princeton, NJ: Princeton University Press, 1999).

47. Ibid., 23–24.

48. Ibid., 29.

49. Frederick Turner, *Beauty: The Value of Values* (Charlottesville and London: University of Virginia Press, 1991), 2ff.

50. Ibid., 3; emphasis in the original.

51. David Bentley Hart, *The Beauty of the Infinite: The Aesthetics of Christian Truth* (Grand Rapids, MI: Eerdmans, 2003), 17–21.

52. Susan A. Ross, "Women, Beauty, and Justice: Moving Beyond von Balthasar," *Journal of the Society of Christian Ethics* 25/1 (Spring/ Summer 2005), 81.

53. Scarry, *On Beauty and Being Just,* 25.

54. For example, Willow Creek Church, in Barrington, Illinois, one of the largest evangelical churches in the country, has as its central place of worship a large auditorium that is deliberately devoid of any religious symbolism. It is intended to look corporate and not religious.

55. Don E. Saliers, *Worship as Theology: Foretaste of Glory Divine* (Nashville: Abingdon Press, 1994), 205, 207.

56. Susan J. White, *A History of Women in Christian Worship* (Cleveland: Pilgrim Press, 2003).

57. Ibid., 1.

58. Sandra J. Schneiders, "The Effect of Women's Experience on Their Spirituality," *Spirituality Today* 35/2 (Summer 1983), 100–116.

59. Code of Canon Law Web page, www.womenpriests.org.

60. Ibid.

61. 1983 Code of Canon Law, Canon 230, 1–3.

62. The 1980 document *Inestimabile Donum* reiterated the instruction that "the faithful, whether religious or lay, who are authorized as extraordinary ministers of the Eucharist can distribute Communion only when there is no priest, deacon, or acolyte; when the priest is impeded by illness or advanced age; or when the number of the faithful going to Communion is so large as to make the celebration of Mass excessively long."

63. Canon Law, Canon 813.

64. http://www.sspxafrica.com/documents/2002
_JunJuly/Restoring_the_Veil.htm.

65. http://www.wff.org/WFFFAQ.html.

66. "The Quiet Heretic," *Chronicle of Higher Education*, August 12, 2005.

67. "On special occasions, the alto part was strengthened by one or two women who did not, however, walk in procession but were concealed behind the choir stalls." See http://www.osp.org.uk/music/choir.htm.

68. Canon 766.

69. Mary Catherine Hilkert, OP, *Speaking with Authority: Catherine of Siena and the Voices of Women Today* (New York: Paulist Press, 2001).

70. See http://www.stjosephsonline.com/rosary_altar_society.htm.

71. Shirley Manigault, in *Crowns: Portraits of Black Women in Church Hats* (New York: Doubleday, 2000), 75.

72. Sherrie Flynt-Wallington, in *Crowns,* 51.

73. Martha Manning, *Chasing Grace: Reflections of a Catholic Girl, Grown Up* (New York: HarperSanFrancisco, 1996), 96.

74. For some representative examples, see, for example, *Women at Worship: Interpretations of North American Diversity,* ed. Marjorie Procter-Smith and Janet R. Walton (Louisville, KY: Westminster John Knox, 1993); Sheila Durkin Dierks, *WomenEucharist* (Boulder, CO: WovenWord Press, 1997); Rosemary Radford

Ruether, *Women-Church: Theology and Practice of Feminist Liturgical Communities* (Boston: Beacon Press, 1985); Charlotte Caron, *To Make and Make Again: Feminist Ritual Thealogy* (New York: Crossroad, 1993).

75. Lesley A. Northup, *Ritualizing Women: Patterns of Spirituality* (Cleveland: Pilgrim Press, 1997), esp. chap. 2, "Emerging Patterns in Women's Ritualizing," 28–52.

76. Janet R. Walton, *Feminist Liturgy: A Matter of Justice* (Collegeville, MN: Liturgical Press, 2000).

77. See my "Women, Beauty, and Justice: Moving Beyond von Balthasar," *Journal of the Society of Christian Ethics* 25/1 (Spring/Summer 2005), 79–98.

78. Elizabeth A. Johnson, *She Who Is: The Mystery of God in Feminist Theological Discourse* (New York: Crossroad, 1992), 3.

79. Ibid., 4–5.

80. See William Cleary, *Prayers to She Who Is* (New York: Crossroad, 1995); the book *She Who Is* includes a number of illustrations, from a reproduction of Michelangelo's Sistine Chapel ceiling to the work of Meinrad Craighead and other contemporary women artists (between pp. 57 and 59 in *She Who Is*). Johnson has commented in lectures that she has received many pictures and poems inspired by her book.

81. Richard John Neuhaus, "In the Beauty of Holiness," *First Things* 75 (August–September 1997), 74.

82. Ibid.

83. Ibid.

84. As quoted in ibid., 74.

85. Ibid., 75.

86. Ibid., 74.

87. I am not alone in my concerns. See Thomas Day, *Why Catholics Can't Sing: The Culture of Catholicism and the Triumph of Bad Taste* (New York: Crossroad, 1990) and the Web site "Society for a Moratorium on the Music of Marty Haugen and David Haas": http://www.mgilleland.com/music/moratorium.htm.

88. "Nevertheless the liturgy is the summit toward which the activity of the Church is directed; at the same time it is the fountain from which all her power flows"; *Sacrosanctum Concilium* (The Sacred Constitution on the Liturgy), 10, in *The Documents of Vatican II*, ed. Walter M. Abbott, SJ (New York: America Press, 1975), 142.

89. Presentation of the Nobel Prize, December 10, 2004, as found at http://www.nobelprize.org.

90. Ibid.

91. Ibid.

92. Ibid.

93. Margaret Courtney-Clarke, *Ndbele: The Art of an African Tribe* (New York: Thames and Hudson, 1986, 2002).

94. Maya Angelou, *My Painted House, My Friendly Chicken, and Me,* with photographs by Margaret Courtney-Clarke (New York: Crown Publishers, 1994).

95. Ibid., n.p.

96. Margaret Courtney-Clarke, *Imazighen: The Vanishing Traditions of Berber Women* (New York: Clarkson Potter, 1996).

97. Ibid., ix.

98. Pamela Sherrod, "The Rhythm of Healing," *Chicago Tribune,* May 11, 2003, Section 15, p. 1.

99. *Imazighen,* xxiv.

100. Scarry, *On Beauty and Being Just,* 111.

101. Certainly an emphasis on humility is true of von Balthasar, who finds in Mary the perfect recipient of the glory of God; see *Mary for Today,* trans. Robert Nowell (San Francisco: Ignatius Press, 1988); my emphasis on humility is somewhat different, however, from von Balthasar's. See Jame Schaeffer, "Appreciating the Beauty of Earth," *Theological Studies* 62, no. 1 (March 2001), 23–52.

102. Valerie Saiving (Goldstein), "Human Experience: A Feminine View," *Journal of Religion* 40 (January 1960), reprinted in *Womanspirit Rising: A Feminist Reader in Religion,* ed. Carol P. Christ and Judith Plaskow (New York: Harper, 1979), 25–42.

103. Judith Plaskow, *Sex, Sin and Grace* (see n. 42 above); Barbara Hilkert Andolsen, "Agape

in feminist Ethics," *Journal of Religious Ethics* 9/1 (Spring 1981): 69–83; Susan Nelson, *Healing the Broken Heart: Sin, Alienation, and the Gift of Grace* (St. Louis, MO: Chalice Press, 1997).

104. For just two examples, see *Violence against Women and Children: A Christian Theological Sourcebook,* ed. Carol J. Adams and Marie M. Fortune (New York: Continuum, 1995); Rita Nakashima Brock, *Journeys by Heart: A Christology of Erotic Power* (New York: Crossroad, 1988).

105. Margaret Farley, "New Patterns of Relationship: Beginnings of a Moral Revolution," in *Theological Studies* 36/4 (December 1975), 627–46; see also her *Personal Commitments,* n. 44 above.

106. See Schaeffer, "Appreciating the Beauty of Earth," 23–52.

107. Thomas Aquinas, *Summa Theologiae,* II–II, q. 161, a. 1.

108. *ST,* II–II, q. 161, a. 2, reply to obj. 3.

109. 161, a.3.

110. 161, a.4.

111. 161, a. 3.

112. *ST* I–II, q. 58.

113. *ST* 161, a. 5.

114. Beverly Wildung Harrison, "Doing Christian Ethics," in *Justice in the Making: Feminist Social Ethics,* ed. Elizabeth M. Bounds et

al. (Louisville and London: Westminster John Knox Press, 2004), 31.

115. Ibid., 36.

116. Ibid., 34.

117. Susan A. Ross, *Extravagant Affections: A Feminist Sacramental Theology* (New York: Continuum, 1998), 46.

118. *ST* III, q. 61, a. 1.

119. Victor Zuckerkandl, quoted in Jeremy Begbie, *Theology, Music and Time* (Cambridge: Cambridge University Press, 2000), 128.

120. Iris Murdoch, *The Sovereignty of Good* (London and New York: Routledge, 1970, 2001), 64.

121. The most popular version of this song was written in Lawrence, Massachusetts, during the mill strikes of 1912. The original lyrics were by James Oppenheim, music is attributed to Martha Coleman and/or Caroline Kohlsaat. See Edith Fowke and Joe Glazer, eds., *Songs of Work and Protest* (New York: Dover, 1973).

The Madeleva Lecture in Spirituality

This series, sponsored by the Center for Spirituality, Saint Mary's College, Notre Dame, Indiana, honors annually the woman who as president of the college inaugurated its pioneering graduate program in theology, Sister M. Madeleva, C.S.C.

1985
Monika K. Hellwig
Christian Women in a Troubled World

1986
Sandra M. Schneiders
Women and the Word

1987
Mary Collins
Women at Prayer

1988
Maria Harris
Women and Teaching

1989
Elizabeth Dreyer
Passionate Women: Two Medieval Mystics

1990
Joan Chittister, OSB
Job's Daughters

1991
Dolores R. Leckey
Women and Creativity

1992
Lisa Sowle Cahill
Women and Sexuality

1993
Elizabeth A. Johnson
Women, Earth, and Creator Spirit

1994
Gail Porter Mandell
Madeleva: One Woman's Life

1995
Diana L. Hayes
Hagar's Daughters

1996
Jeanette Rodriguez
Stories We Live
Cuentos Que Vivimos

1997
Mary C. Boys
Jewish-Christian Dialogue

1998
Kathleen Norris
The Quotidian Mysteries

1999
Denise Lardner Carmody
An Ideal Church: A Meditation

2000
Sandra M. Schneiders
With Oil in Their Lamps

2001
Mary Catherine Hilkert
Speaking with Authority

2002
Margaret A. Farley
Compassionate Respect

2003
Sidney Callahan
Women Who Hear Voices

2004
Mary Ann Hinsdale, IHM
Women Shaping Theology

[No Lecture in 2005]